THE FALLACIOUS BELIEF IN GOVERNMENT

Warp Speed Toward Tyranny

JEFFREY HANN

Journalistic Revolution

Copyright © 2025 Journalistic Revolution

All rights reserved.

No part of this book may be reproduced, in any manner, without written permission from the publisher or author, except for the use of brief quotations in book or article reviews.

Paperback: 979-8-9874490-3-5
Ebook: 979-8-9874490-4-2

Library of Congress Control Number: 2025900438

First edition March 2025

Published by:
Journalistic Revolution, LLC
PO Box 130
Eatonville, WA 98328

https://www.journalisticrevolution.com

Table of Contents

Preface 1
Critical Thinking: A Simplified Breakdown 4
Lifecycle of Government 22
Protect and Serve: Reality 33
Constitutional Contradictions 43
Education as a Tool of Indoctrination 58
Taxation is Theft 67
Engineered Consent 85
Psychological Operations 93
Conspiracy Theories 116
Anarchism with Facilitating Systems 157
About the Author 177

Preface

"*Evolution, as we understand it, and as it must be studied by the human intellect, is the story of the evolution of consciousness, and not the story of the evolution of the form. This latter evolution is implicit in the other, and of secondary importance from the occult angle.*" – Alice Bailey, *A Treatise on the Seven Rays: Volume 2: Esoteric Psychology II* (1941)

    This book culminates a decade-long journey of critical analysis, in-depth research, and a relentless pursuit of truth. This path has led me to understand and identify the root cause of humanity's issues. Keeping it in an endless cycle of insanity and perpetual control through violence, coercion, and force. The next evolutionary progression in front of humanity is not physical but of the mind and consciousness. I didn't set out to make this determination but to correct the rhetoric I thought was true based on the education I had growing up. Little did I know the ramifications of this path and pursuit or the vision of humanity's future that would begin to take shape for me. This book will challenge deeply ingrained beliefs, expose the fallacy of government as a necessary evil, and show humanity's only path toward a freer, more self-governing future. At its core, it's not merely an argument against the idea of government but a call to all individuals to think critically and independently -as a skill set- embracing systems that promote voluntary cooperation and exchange.

    This journey toward evolutionary progress begins with the Trivium Method of Critical Thinking (Trivium), an ancient framework and workflow for understanding reality through three pillars: Grammar, Logic, and Rhetoric. Grammar is where we gather accurate data and understand the facts of a given situation; Logic is where we analyze those facts and identify contradictions and fallacies; and Rhetoric equips us to express our conclusions and desired actions effectively. This foundational structure and process, particularly the Trivium, is our shield against propaganda, emotional manipulation, and fallacious reasoning -impactful tools governments use to maintain control. Starting with the Trivium is critical because it provides the intellectual protection and wisdom to discern truth in a world of deceptive, unethical, and immoral behavior and act with understanding and insight.

Intelligence alone is not enough to navigate the complexities of life or solve humanity's most significant challenges. Actual progress requires the wisdom to act upon the knowledge and intelligence gained in ways that align with ethical and moral principles. Wisdom, as the bridge between knowing and doing, enables us to evaluate when and how to apply our skill sets effectively. This difference is essential to understand; while intelligence builds knowledge and can identify a problem or an opportunity, wisdom ensures that our actions align with principles and ethical considerations. Without the balance between intelligence and wisdom and metacognition -thinking about thinking- even the most brilliant minds can be misled or manipulated, stressing the importance of cultivating knowledge with purpose.

Central to the message of this book is the declaration that the belief in government is a fallacy. Throughout history, governments have claimed to act in the public's best interest while systematically exploiting and consolidating power to benefit the few at the expense of the many. From taxation to manufactured crises that expand government control, the patterns are clear: the government consolidates power under the appearance of safety and service, violating the freedoms it purports to protect. Understanding and accepting this reality is not an act of treasonous rebellion but liberation from the metaphysical chains placed upon us since birth. It frees us from these cognitive chains that bind us to systems of control and opens the door to a brighter future.

This book is not just a diagnosis of the root cause of our problems but a roadmap to solutions that respect natural rights, promote voluntaryism, and foster societies built around sustainable, free, and organized communities. It delves into concepts like facilitatism, offering practical tools for decentralized problem-solving and voluntary cooperation and exchange. It paints a vision of a society where individuals are not ruled by tyranny and violence but empowered by systems that serve as tools for coordination and collaboration. It presents alternatives to the tools and actions of control that currently dictate our lives.

The stakes are high, with dangerous threats at every step. Humanity is at a crossroads where the expansion of centralized power threatens to destroy individual freedoms and rights worldwide in a new Age of Tyranny. Yet, there is hope. By dismantling the fallacious belief in government and equipping ourselves with critical thinking skills through the Trivium, we can break free from the endless cycles of Tyranny and chart a new course toward humanity's evolution. This book is a beacon and call for us to question, challenge, and evolve beyond the Tyranny that has controlled us for millennia. The future of humanity depends on our willingness to confront these truths and take defiant action in the face of a growing tyranny unseen in written history. Each of us has a role in shaping this future, or we will continue in an endless cycle of insanity.

"The most merciful thing in the world, I think, is the inability of the human mind to correlate all its contents. We live on a placid island of ignorance in the midst of black seas of infinity, and it was not meant that we should voyage far. The sciences, each straining in its own direction, have hitherto harmed us little; but some day the piecing together of dissociated knowledge will open up such terrifying vistas of reality, and of our frightful position therein, that we shall either go mad from the revelation or flee from the light into the peace and safety of a new dark age." – Howard Phillips Lovecraft, *The Call of Cthulhu* (1926)

Critical Thinking: A Simplified Breakdown

"The smart way to keep people passive and obedient is to strictly limit the spectrum of acceptable opinion, but allow very lively debate within that spectrum—even encourage the more critical and dissident views. That gives people the sense that there's free thinking going on, while all the time the presuppositions of the system are being reinforced by the limits put on the range of the debate." – Noam Chomsky, *The Common Good* (1998)

The journey to critical thinking is a path of intellectual empowerment, a transformative concept of perpetual self-growth, and a skill set that should be wielded daily and in all situations. This development is not just essential but also invaluable to the evolution of humanity. However, it's a skill that's typically overlooked in government-run education. **Could this be due to ulterior motives, or is it a result of a lack of understanding of critical thinking?**

The first thing we need to understand is the definition of critical thinking, and then we need to be aware of the process by which we conduct critical thinking, metacognition. Anyone can have an innate ability to think critically, but that is not the same as developing a skill set based on repeatable and efficient processes.

Critical thinking *is skillfully defining, intellectualizing, analyzing, and evaluating data and information gathered from all sources and producing belief and action in rhetoric that provides clarity and consistency through evidence and reason.*

Grammar (Input)

What is a grammar? What is a word? Why does it matter that we share a common understanding of words and their definitions? What does it mean to communicate with others? How do we express our feelings and emotions to those we care about? Does it matter if others understand the words we use? How can we grow as a society if we do not know what is being discussed amongst ourselves? Can we identify what objective versus subjective is? How do we gather and compile data in a structured way? These questions describe the importance of understanding the definitions of words -the intent- behind the communication.

Grammar, "the art of letters," is a structured set and systematic account of rules about words and phrases and the meaning behind them in an understandable format -words have objective meanings. Within the Trivium, the pillar of Grammar is the "input" phase, where we methodically and coherently gather factual data in its root and raw, semi-structured, and structured forms -knowledge gathered and organized into various categories that can be analyzed individually and holistically.

Grammar is where we gather root and modern definitions, themes, and context around the data. It is the place where objective reality is separated from subjective reality. This is where we answer the questions about a subject: Who, What, Where, and When. It is a place where we order the evidence into a systematic knowledge base. This systematic body of knowledge is the source of the pillar of Rhetoric. As new information is presented, it must be checked against the body of knowledge that has been previously collected to determine if it changes anything. Debating cannot start and end in the world of Rhetoric unless the goal is to control and manipulate others. The goal is to create a robust knowledge base that can be further analyzed and applied to real-world situations, stimulating our intellect and making us well-prepared and knowledgeable for any situation.

Critical Thinking: A Simplified Breakdown

Objective vs. Subjective Truths

We must understand the differences between objective and subjective truths to ensure that a subject's systematic knowledge base is factual and comprehensive, providing more accurate Rhetoric. Objective truths are based on observable and verifiable facts, have universal validity, and are supported by repeatable and testable empirical evidence. They are unbiased, free from personal interpretations, and consistently produce similar results under comparable conditions. They provide a solid foundation for Rhetoric, where we use this knowledge to persuade and influence others.

Examples
- Water will freeze at 0°C or 32°F under standard atmospheric pressure
- United States (U.S.) Declaration of Independence was signed in 1776

Subjective truths are inherently personal and vary between individuals. They have relative validity, meaning they may be true for one person but not others because they are rooted in an emotional basis: personal feelings, opinions, and judgments. They evolve as individuals gain new experiences or insights throughout life, which leads to their subjective views.

Examples
- Chocolate is the best ice cream flavor
- This movie is a masterpiece and the greatest of all time

Objective and subjective data can overlap, particularly in psychology, sociology, or ethics. For example, in psychology, an individual's subjective experience is considered alongside objective measurements to understand mental health. In sociology, the objective reality of social structures is interpreted through the subjective experiences of individuals, providing individual insight into actions. In ethics, objective principles are applied to subjective situations to determine potential violations. Recognizing the differences between these truths helps us approach the Trivium with greater confidence that our Rhetoric will be accurate and balanced. It allows us to respect factual realities and personal viewpoints while cleanly organizing our structured knowledge base. This will lead to more effective communication, better decision-making and problem-solving, and a deeper appreciation of the human experience and social interaction.

Definitions and Semantics

Language is a potent tool with the unique ability to unite, divide, enlighten, or deceive. Its influence transcends mere expression, serving as a communication medium that can shape social dynamics and sometimes cause devastating effects. Definitions and words' meanings are essential to understanding and communication. **How do we communicate effectively without understanding the definition of a word and having that shared experience of understanding?**

Definitions are pivotal in resolving disputes, evaluating ethical violations, and establishing a shared reality of understanding that provides a common ground on which all parties can stand. However, the sophist's manipulation of language -*a practice of using clever but false arguments and deceptive reasoning*- can distort meaning and twist truths, ultimately resulting in conflicts and confusion that cause individuals to act against their intended desires. Recognizing the distinctions between root and modern definitions and interpretations and understanding the dangers of sophistry is crucial for fostering honest dialogue and critical thinking.

Root definitions of words are derived from the etymology and original usage in a particular historical or cultural context and are crucial in understanding a word's accurate meaning. These definitions provide a starting point for the objective meaning of a word before it evolves through time, culture, and subjective interpretation. Root definitions strip away modern biases and interpretations, exposing the essence of a term. This process is vital when engaging in debates, ethical discussions, or analysis, as it forces individuals to establish a shared understanding, facilitating honest dialogue. If we cannot agree upon a definition of a term, then effective communication is difficult to obtain.

As societies rise and fall, so does language. Modern definitions usually reflect the cultural, social, or political trends of the time. While this evolution can enrich language, it can lead to inconsistencies and contradictions, especially when words are weaponized for ideological purposes and control. Modern definitions typically face subjectivity based on cultural norms and cognitive biases that can distort their meaning. Additionally, words frequently acquire multiple meanings over time, leading to ambiguity and making their interpretation heavily dependent on context. This opens the door for sophist manipulation, where definitions are strategically altered to influence thought, shape policy, or sway public opinion. Root definitions ensure that debates remain anchored in shared understanding rather than subjective whims.

Example
- **Root Definition**: '**Patriot**,' from the Latin *patriota* and Greek *patriotes*, meaning "fellow-countryman" or "one who supports their fatherland." Country means "landmass controlled by a government." In the 18th century, 'patriot' also carried a more controversial connotation as "a factious disturber of the government," a term used to describe those fighting for independence during the American Revolution.
- **Modern Interpretation**: An individual who energetically supports their country and is prepared to defend it against enemies or detractors. The term is associated with unwavering loyalty to national identity and symbols.

- **Implications**: The root and modern definition emphasizes shared loyalty to one's homeland and government, grounded in unity and cultural identity. However, its historical usage during the American Revolution as a label for dissenters shows the distinction between allegiance to the government and resistance to tyranny and those who challenged authority and tyranny in pursuit of freedom and natural rights.

The term '**sophistry**' is usually cloaked in plausible rhetoric to manipulate opinions and obscure objective truths, posing a significant threat to honest dialogue and the pursuit of truth. Fallacious arguments are logically flawed or misleading and used to deceive or manipulate. The term originates from the Greek *sophistes*, meaning "wise man" or "expert," but evolved quickly to denote those who use misleading arguments for personal gain. Socrates, Plato, and Aristotle expressed their disdain for sophists. Sophists typically twist language by redefining terms to suit their agendas, creating confusion or presenting false equivalence that distorts understanding. They use emotional manipulation rather than logical reasoning to manipulate others, appealing to sentiments rather than facts. They deliberately use vague language, enabling them to evade accountability or mislead their audience. Recognizing and maintaining caution against sophistry is crucial to preserving objective truth and having a meaningful and honest dialogue.

Semantics is the study of meaning in language and plays an essential role in critical thinking. Without clear definitions, meaningful dialogue and debate are impossible. The Trivium emphasizes starting with accurate, objective definitions before analyzing and discussing a specific topic. Debates that focus solely on Rhetoric, as politicians do, without addressing the pillars of Grammar and Logic, often devolve into misunderstandings or manipulations, which can have catastrophic effects.

Context and Themes

Context and themes are key aspects shaping the understanding and interpretation of definitions and language. Context provides the situational background, circumstances, and cues that inform how words and phrases should be interpreted and meant. Immediate context refers to the direct situation where communication happens, such as the different meanings of "run" in sports, software, or elections. Cultural and social context involves the influence of cultural norms and idioms, like "breaking the ice," which might not translate universally. Historical context shows how word meanings evolve due to social changes, such as "gay" shifting from meaning "happy" to referring to sexual orientation or beyond. Relational context emphasizes how relationships between speakers affect interpretation; for example, sarcasm from a friend might be humorous, but the same from a stranger could seem offensive. Understanding these contexts provides information and awareness in communication.

Themes are the underlying ideas or messages for a specific topic, and they play a crucial role in creating a sense of connection and emotional engagement. They provide cohesion and focus by accentuating the central ideas or messages being addressed, acting as an adhesive that binds different pieces of information together. By setting the tone and influencing how information is received and remembered, themes foster a sense of connection and emotional engagement, making others feel more involved in the communication process.

While the interplay between context and themes is evident in effective communication strategies, it's important to note that applying these elements can also present challenges. For example, in a multicultural setting, understanding the cultural context of each individual can be complex and time-consuming. A well-crafted speech adapts its message to the context of the audience -considering their cultural, social, and historical background- while centering the discourse around a compelling theme. Similarly, in persuasive writing or advertising, themes evoke emotions and align the readers with the desired rhetoric. However, only when paired with proper context does the message land successfully.

Logic (Processing)

Logic, the second pillar of the Trivium, is the analytical phase where raw, semi-structured, and structured data collected during Grammar is meticulously scrutinized and refined. Its primary role is to eliminate inherent and external paradoxes, fallacies, and biases, ensuring clarity and coherence in understanding and reasoning. This process evaluates information's validity and resolves contradictions, transforming knowledge into understanding. Logic bridges Grammar and Rhetoric, shaping sound and compelling conclusions. By rigorously applying Logic, individuals protect themselves from manipulation, encourage self-awareness, and contribute to reasoned discourse.

Logic is a tool for navigating complex realities and is key to developing intellectual and ethical growth. As information is refined, a systematic understanding of the subject emerges, laying the groundwork for Rhetoric. Effective rhetoric is contingent on sound logic; without it, even factual, objective evidence may struggle to persuade or enlighten others. By emphasizing the role of Logic in navigating complex realities, we can feel more equipped for intellectual and ethical growth.

Derived from the Greek word *logos*, meaning "word, reason, speech, or idea," Logic stresses the relationship between words and their meanings. To process reality effectively, logical reasoning must be grounded in objective truth, ensuring that language semantics do not obscure understanding. Without this process, confusion will persist, leading to flawed conclusions. When correctly applied, Logic reflects the principles of reality, allowing us to discern the "why" of any subject and achieve a systematic understanding of reality.

Logic is a tool for personal growth, as it requires introspection to identify and correct our inherent paradoxes, deductive and inductive reasoning, logical fallacies, inherent contradictions, and cognitive biases. For example, when examining our personal beliefs, we can use Logic to ensure they are based on sound reasoning and evidence rather than emotional or social influences. Similarly, when engaging in external arguments, we can apply logical principles to evaluate the arguments and counterarguments critically, ensuring a rational and well-informed discussion. Logical principles should be used for our personal beliefs and external arguments, providing a path for refining our critical thinking skill set and enhancing our capacity to engage meaningfully with the world. When new information arises, Logic prompts a return to Grammar to reassess the knowledge base, ensuring an iterative and evolving understanding of truth. This process of introspection and correction is a key part of the Trivium, making Logic an essential tool for self-improvement.

Paradoxes

Paradoxes are statements or situations that appear self-contradictory but usually reveal deeper truths upon examination. Logic seeks to resolve such contradictions by analyzing the context and semantics of statements and differentiating between objective and subjective truths. Paradoxes often arise from sophistry or careless rhetoric, making logical scrutiny indispensable.

Example
- **Epimenides Paradox**, "All Cretans are liars," spoken by a Cretan. **Are they lying or telling the truth?** This shows the complexities of language and subjective interpretation of a string of words conveying meaning.

Critical Thinking: A Simplified Breakdown

Deductive and Inductive Reasoning

Western logic, formalized by Aristotle, introduced syllogism -a deductive reasoning framework based on propositions deemed true or false. Deductive reasoning ensures that conclusions are undoubtedly true if the premises are valid. Inductive reasoning yields probable conclusions based on observed patterns, which may vary in strength and accuracy -conclusions are not absolute.

Examples
- **Deductive reasoning** – "All humans are mortal. Socrates is human. Therefore, Socrates is mortal."
- **Inductive reasoning** – "During crises, governments expand their power through emergency declarations and militarized forces, then fight to retain it by suppressing dissent and disobedience. Therefore, crises drive governments toward Tyranny."

Logical Fallacies

Logical fallacies, formal or informal, are reasoned thoughts and statements with defects in the logical structure that mislead and deceive those receiving the statements. The difference between the formal and informal variants is that informal fallacies are valid in form but have one or more false premises, making the conclusion false. Recognizing and avoiding these pitfalls is possible and central to Logic. For every way to think of something, there is a potential fallacy that can go with it.

Examples
- **Ad hominem** – Attacking the person instead of the argument.

- "We shouldn't listen to her climate change proposal because she doesn't recycle!"
- **Appeal to authority** – Relying on authority figures without questioning their claims.
  - "The CEO of a major tech company said this new app is revolutionary, so it must be true!"
- **Strawman** – Misrepresenting an opponent's argument to refute it more easily.
  - "You believe people should have the right to own guns? So, you're okay with everyone carrying weapons in schools!"
- **Appeal to emotion** – Manipulating emotions instead of presenting evidence.
  - "If we don't pass this law immediately, imagine how many innocent children could suffer!"
- **Broken Window Fallacy** – Illustrating flawed reasoning in economics.
  - "The hurricane damaged homes, creating construction jobs, which is great for the economy!"

Inherent Contradictions

Inherent contradictions arise when a concept, system, or argument contains internal inconsistencies, reducing rationality. Identifying and addressing these contradictions is challenging due to our innate need to be correct and our unwillingness to admit holding contradicting truths. These contradictions reveal underlying flaws, exposing gaps between theory and practice or intention and outcome, and by addressing them, we can overcome the challenges driving us toward personal growth.

Critical Thinking: A Simplified Breakdown 17

Examples
- **Freedom and Regulation** – The concept of a "free market" typically coexists with extensive regulation, creating a contradiction between economic freedom and government intervention.
  - Advocating for free trade while enforcing tariffs and subsidies contradicts the claim of economic freedom.
- **Equality Under the Law** – Legal systems emphasize equality, yet systemic disparities in enforcement or access to justice reveal inherent contradictions.
  - A country may proclaim equality in its constitution while maintaining laws or practices that disproportionately affect marginalized groups.
- **War for Peace** – Justifying military interventions as a means to achieve peace presents an inherent contradiction, as the very act of war disrupts the stability it claims to restore.
  - A government engages in prolonged foreign conflicts under the pretense of establishing democracy and freedom, leading to further unrest and authoritarian outcomes.

Cognitive Biases

Cognitive biases arise from mental shortcuts, known as heuristics, that simplify decision-making processes and are typically unconscious acts that most are unaware of. These heuristics can be practical and efficient in day-to-day problem-solving applications but can lead to flawed conclusions if not critically examined. These biases shape how we interpret data, favoring speed and simplicity over accuracy and depth of reasoning. Identifying and addressing biases is essential for cultivating sound reasoning and our critical thinking skill set.

Examples
- **Confirmation Bias** – Favoring information supporting pre-existing beliefs while disregarding evidence contradicting them.
    - Someone convinced that a political candidate is honest focuses on news stories highlighting the candidate's integrity while ignoring behavior or ethical concerns.
- **Hindsight Bias** – Overestimating an ability to predict an event after it has occurred.
    - Initially supported the COVID19 lockdowns, then later claimed they "always knew" the restrictions were excessive and harmful to society.
- **Availability Bias** – Estimating the likelihood of an event based on the ease of examples recalled from recent occurrences in our memory.
    - Mainstream media pushes COVID19 lockdowns and mandates as effective and necessary, causing people to believe it is true despite evidence suggesting that such measures cause significant economic and social harm.
- **Sunk Cost Fallacy** – Continuing to invest in a decision or project based on prior investments, even when it is no longer rational.
    - The government continues to fund a failing infrastructure project despite its inefficiency and escalating costs because it has already spent billions of taxpayer dollars, and it would be a "waste" if it ended the project.
- **Groupthink** – When a group prioritizes cohesion and consensus over critical analysis, leading to flawed decisions and actions. Individuals may unconsciously align their views with the group's prevailing opinion, even if it contradicts their personal beliefs or better judgment, to avoid disrupting unity or facing social rejection.

Critical Thinking: A Simplified Breakdown

- A team might unanimously agree on a flawed business strategy because no one wants to challenge the leader's opinion, even if they have valid concerns.

Rhetoric (Output)

Rhetoric, the final pillar of the Trivium, is the art of effectively communicating ideas derived from the analytical processes of Grammar and Logic. It empowers us to bridge understanding and action, emphasizing clear, persuasive, and ethical expression. Rhetoric enables us to share information, inspire others, drive meaningful discussions, and encourage informed decision-making. It distinguishes itself as a tool for connection and influence, vital in turning knowledge into impactful outcomes. Rhetoric, as we know it today, started with Aristotle's stand against sophistry, specifically Isocrates' work on Rhetoric in trying to create the perfect city-state citizen. Aristotle viewed Rhetoric as having three means of persuasion: Ethos, Pathos, and Logos. Ethos is our habitual character, beliefs, morals, and ideals at an individual and community level. Pathos is the potential pain and suffering of the experience of going through something and the appeals made to the emotion and ideals of that experience. Logos is our speech, discourse, and accounts of situations tempered with reason and understanding.

Rhetoric within the Trivium aims to persuade, enlighten, and ethically inspire, nurturing understanding and respect. Politicians use rhetoric as a tool for manipulation, seeking to deceive or control for selfish or nefarious purposes. It's not just about the message but the ethical and moral implications of its delivery. Tailoring messages to resonate with others' unique and subjective perspectives is essential for effective rhetoric and discourse. The receivers of rhetoric are not just passive recipients but active participants who are integral to the communication process. For example, a healthcare advocate addressing medical professionals might use technical language and detailed statistics; however, speaking to the general public might involve relatable stories and simplified explanations of the benefits.

Rhetoric isn't just about presenting ideas; it's about inspiring action and driving meaningful change with words based on proper Grammar and Logic. If it doesn't have proper Grammar and Logic, chances are it is being used to manipulate and control -to govern us. Effective rhetoric can transform complex information into clear, compelling messages that resonate with others and inspire them to take specific steps. It bridges the gap between understanding and application, ensuring that the insights derived from Grammar and Logic lead to tangible and actionable outcomes. When providing calls to action, Rhetoric must be well-defined, realistic, and supported by evidence, making it easier for individuals or groups to act confidently and decisively. When this occurs, Rhetoric becomes a powerful tool for informing and mobilizing individuals and evolving society toward positive transformations.

The Trivium functions as an interconnected blueprint for critical thinking, with each stage and pillar enhancing the effectiveness of the next. Grammar is the foundation, collecting raw, semi-structured, and structured data, objective and subjective truths, and definitions essential for understanding a topic. This pillar ensures that information and data are accurate and contextualized, providing a solid base for deeper analysis and processing. Logic then refines this knowledge base, scrutinizing the data for paradoxes, fallacies, contradictions, and biases and evaluating the validity of the conclusions, ensuring that the information and data are accurate and logically sound. Finally, Rhetoric transforms these supported conclusions, based on evidence and reason, into effective communication, presenting ideas persuasively and ethically to drive understanding and action.

If new information changes our rhetoric, then so be it. **We want the truth, correct?** We must accept that we could be wrong and be willing

Critical Thinking: A Simplified Breakdown

to move from deeply held beliefs and biases to seek our reality's truth. We should trust in our ability to learn critical thinking as a skill set, but it starts with the understanding that we must address our logical fallacies and hard-held beliefs. Everyone has fallacies and errors in their thought processes, believing in things that are not factually true, so it is up to us to correct our thought processes.

The Trivium transcends traditional approaches by emphasizing self-awareness, metacognition, intellectual discipline, and ethical and effective communication. This allows us to make informed decisions based on accurate, analyzed information while resisting manipulative and controlling rhetoric. In an age of information overload, the Trivium provides the tool to discern truth from falsehood, ensuring that individuals can approach challenges with clarity and confidence. It is a practical and relevant structure for understanding and interacting with reality. As we work towards mastering the Trivium, we cultivate a lifelong skill set that enhances personal growth, fosters ethical communication, and contributes to informed and just societies.

"He is the best of all who thinks for himself in all things. He, too, is good who takes advice from a wiser (person). But he who neither thinks for himself, nor lays to heart another's wisdom, this is a useless man." – Aristotle, *The Ethics Of Aristotle (Vol. I)*, translated by Arthur Humphreys (1902)

Lifecycle of Government

"Those who belong to this small class have tasted how sweet and blessed a possession philosophy is, and have also seen enough of the madness of the multitude; and they know that no politician is honest, nor is there any champion of justice at whose side they may fight and be saved. Such an one may be compared to a man who has fallen among wild beasts -- he will not join in the wickedness of his fellows, but neither is he able singly to resist all their fierce natures, and therefore seeing that he would be of no use to the State or to his friends, and reflecting that he would have to throw away his life without doing any good either to himself or others, he holds his peace, and goes his own way. He is like one who, in the storm of dust and sleet which the driving wind hurries along, retires under the shelter of a wall; and seeing the rest of mankind full of wickedness, he is content, if only he can live his own life and be pure from evil or unrighteousness, and depart in peace and good-will, with bright hopes." – Plato, *The Republic, Book VI* (375 BC)

The term '**government**' derives from the Latin word *gubernare*, meaning "to steer or control," combined with the suffix *-ment*, signifying a tool or action, which defines government as a "tool or action of control." Now, ask yourself, **can individuals who have not committed any crimes or wrongdoings be free if controlled?**

This root meaning reveals its role as a system that directs and regulates free individuals within a society. Modern interpretations, however, depict government as an entity that manages public policies and social rules, portraying it as a service for the public's safety and welfare, *for the people by the people*. The government has grown to provide healthcare, education, and infrastructure for all. While the government is presented as a system for promoting the collective benefit through a theoretical social contract, this is a false equivalence. When critically analyzed, this false equivalence raises questions about its alignment with individual freedoms and rights. The inherent tension between control and service shows a contradiction within the concept and idea of government. At its core, government remains a tool for controlling social behavior, exerting authority over individual self-rule. This duality has been a constant theme of philosophical inquiry, debating whether the government protects natural rights or is a tool of violent control.

The term '**authority**' derives from the Latin term *auctoritatem*, meaning "invention, advice, opinion, influence, command," and from *auctor*, meaning "master, leader, author," and in context with government, referring to the legitimate power to make decisions and enforce obedience. Modern usage of authority indicates the right or power to enforce rules and policies -give orders- or make decisions, typically attributed to governments, institutions, or individuals in rulership positions. It is stated that governments derive their authority from the "consent of the governed," rooted and enshrined in democratic principles. However, this idea is a fallacy when critically analyzed. By its nature, true authority over the innocent requires voluntary and individual consent, which cannot be assumed from the mere existence of a governing system. Being born does not imply consent to be governed by strangers. The only genuine form of authority is parental or guardianship authority, exercised over children or dependents who cannot yet care for themselves. This authority arises from a natural duty of care and nurturance, unlike the coercive authority governments claim as its domain, which relies on the implicit or forced compliance of individuals who may never have consented to their rule. This distinction emphasizes the philosophical and ethical contradictions inherent in governmental authority, such as the tension between individual autonomy and natural rights and the collective governance we are forced to participate in.

Natural rights -**Life, Freedom, and Property**- are inherent and inalienable in all of humanity and exist independently of laws or governments. Natural rights are rooted in the principles of equality and morality. The Right to Life affirms that every individual has the intrinsic claim to exist without interference or harm from others. The Right to Freedom encompasses self-rule over one's choices and actions, provided they do not violate and infringe upon the rights of others. The Right to Property is tied directly to one's labor and efforts and the right to own, use, trade, and benefit from the fruits of that labor. Natural rights should form the ethical foundation for a just and free society through voluntary cooperation and exchange. When these natural rights are upheld, individuals are empowered to live in harmony with others, free from coercion and oppression.

The concept of being '**free**' originates from the natural right and idea of freedom of movement, representing an unrestrained state where one is neither in bondage nor constrained, physically or metaphysically, and able to act, think, and exist according to one's own will. Freedom of movement reflects a state of self-determination, where imposed barriers do not constrain individuals, whether they are social constructs or governmental controls. Within this context, the tension between natural rights and collective social governance, with the control systems inherent in government, becomes apparent.

Government is the institutionalized and "legally" binding authority over free individuals, supposedly intended to maintain order and resolve conflicts, serving the collective good. One of the most profound analyses focusing on government comes from Plato's *Republic*, where he outlines the cyclical revolution of government through five regimes: Aristocracy, Timocracy, Oligarchy, Democracy, and Tyranny. Plato's model discusses the government's inherent instability and tendency to devolve through dysfunction, leading to revolution and a return to earlier forms of statism. Hence, government has a lifecycle; it is never static and should not be treated as such.

Lifecycle of Government

Plato's Five Regimes

Plato's five regimes present a progression of various stages of government, each embodying distinct values, strengths, and weaknesses. This progress illustrates the cyclical nature of government and the political systems it can come in. Flaws in one system give rise to the next in a repetitive cycle that always ends in Tyranny. This pattern emphasizes centralized power structures' inherent weaknesses and fallacious nature, where corruption and abuse are inevitable over time. The inevitability of Tyranny in Plato's model should raise concerns about the long-term stability of any form of government.

Aristocracy (Rule of the Wise)

Aristocracy is the "ideal" form of government, ruled by philosopher-kings. These philosopher-kings are not just rulers with intellectual competence but individuals who have undergone rigorous philosophical training and deeply understand justice, virtue, and moral integrity. They focus on wisdom, virtue, and moral integrity and rule by ethical guidance and decisions rooted in reason rather than self-interest. The emphasis on philosophical training for rulers in Aristocracy should make us realize the importance of intellectual leadership in positions of power and government, which is severely lacking today.

Timocracy (Rule of the Honorable)

Timocracy arises when pursuing honor and military achievement, replacing virtue and wisdom as the central tenets of government. This shift is significant as it marks a departure from the intellectual and moral characteristics found in philosopher-kings. Instead, social values in Timocracy emphasize discipline, courage, and patriotism *-fellow-*

countryman- producing strong defensive capabilities. The overemphasis on honor creates a rigid, militarized society where intellectual and virtuous pursuits are stifled. The obsession with status and competition leads to materialism, weakening Timocracy and allowing wealth to become the dominant factor in government. This shift moves the government towards Oligarchy.

Oligarchy (Rule of the Wealthy)

An Oligarchy government is represented by a small group of wealthy elites prioritizing their economic interests over the broader population's needs. Its strength lies in economic stability and efficiency in making decisions. However, the concentration of wealth creates severe inequality, resentment, and class divisions, further driving shifts to another stage. Social unrest builds as the rich grow richer and the poor are excluded from power. Feeling the weight of this inequality, the masses eventually demand more significant representation, pushing the government towards Democracy.

Democracy (Rule of the Many)

Democracy is said to celebrate freedom, equality, and popular rule, granting citizens "equal" voices in government and encouraging diversity, innovation, and the expression of individual rights. However, Plato warns that excessive freedom can lead to chaos and oppression. Without a balance between natural rights and discipline, values diminish, and selfish desires overshadow communal responsibilities. This creates fertile ground for demagogues -*rulers manipulating public emotions to gain power*- and opens the door for Tyranny. In truth, Democracy is a wolf in sheep's clothing where the majority enslaves the minority, and it always leads to Tyranny.

Lifecycle of Government

Tyranny (Rule of the One)

Tyranny emerges when rulers exploit the chaos of a failing Democracy to consolidate power, using the appearance of restoring stability and rights for the benefit of citizens as justification. Tyranny is late-stage government -the final stage and conclusion of the government's never-ending lifecycle. Tyranny is marked by systemic abuse, oppression, and the significant loss of natural rights. Tyrants suppress dissent and disobedience, dismantle checks and balances, and rule through fear and violence. When the oppression becomes unbearable, rebellion is sparked, and the eventual overthrow of the regime begins, resulting in a revolution. The ensuing revolution resets the cycle, returning the masses to earlier forms of statism. **Where do you think the U.S. is in its government lifecycle?**

Transitioning to Tyranny

While the U.S. has long been celebrated as a beacon of democracy, it was created initially as a Constitutional Republic -a mixture of several regimes; key developments over these last few decades demonstrate the urgent and gradual destruction of democratic ideals and the creeping emergence of authoritarian oppression. Plato observed a direct correlation and causation driven by democracy's focus on freedoms, pushing the government toward Tyranny. The greater the freedom and liberty achieved for a society, the greater the tyranny that follows. This analysis resonates with the U.S.'s evolution from the 1990s through the 2010s, stressing the need for immediate attention.

Rapid technological advancement and cultural changes during the 1990s promoted freedom and rights for those marginalized by the government. The internet brought unprecedented and unrestricted access to information and data. However, this freedom led to an abundance of government regulations. The 2010s saw the internet shift from a tool for collective growth to a platform where echo chambers flourished, reinforcing individual biases and fallacies, and where the government started using it as a tool of control and information gathering.

In the early 2000s, the post-September 11th, 2001 attacks (9/11) era created fertile ground for rulers to exploit public fear and emotions. Charismatic politicians used "patriotic" rhetoric to consolidate power and justify sweeping changes for the benefit of society. The Patriot Act, enacted in the name of national security, expanded government surveillance powers while curtailing individual rights. Promoted as a necessary response to terrorism, these measures obstructed democratic principles by prioritizing government control over individual rights.

During the democratic stage of the government's lifecycle, the U.S. shifted toward economic policies promoting globalization, leading to economic disparities. By the 2000s, the wealth gap had widened, with the top 1% controlling an increasingly disproportionate share of resources. The middle class faced stagnating wages and declining economic mobility. This declining middle class has continued to shrink, leading to today. This growing inequality fueled resentment, particularly after the 2008 financial crisis, when government bailouts for large corporations while those in the low and middle class had to manage the manufactured crisis without help. Movements like Occupy Wall Street reflected this growing resentment and public anger, but the lack of systemic change deepened the issues. This frustration created fertile ground for authoritarian solutions that the government and its agents provided, with some calling for a larger government to "fix" the system it broke -the Broken Window Fallacy.

Demagoguery -*rulers who appeal to emotions and prejudice to obtain power*- intensified in the 2010s with populist rulers who capitalized on economic frustration and cultural division, e.g., President Obama and President Trump. Politicians on all sides increasingly employed rhetoric that focused on emotional appeals rather than reasoned and evidence-based discourse, promising to restore the U.S.'s

Lifecycle of Government

greatness or protect it from external and internal threats, such as "Hope and Change" or "Make America Great Again." While effective in mobilizing the masses in support, these tactics lead the government closer to Tyranny.

As democratic principles faltered under the weight of inequality, instability, and division, the stage is set for a ruler to emerge as a supposed savior fighting against the oppressive rule of tyranny. The rise of populism in the 2010s exemplified this dynamic and focus. Political rhetoric increasingly framed dissent and disobedience as unpatriotic or dangerous, normalizing the curtailing of freedoms and support of tyranny.

The expansion of executive power across multiple administrations and the grinding down of checks and balances stresses the shift from Democracy to Tyranny. For example, concentrating and abusing authority in the presidency through executive orders to bypass legislative gridlock became more frequent. In the case of combating terrorism, the use of indiscriminate drone strikes and indefinite detention without trial demonstrates how the pursuit of security comes at the expense of principles, ethics, and morals. Whatever the government is willing to use against others, it is willing to use against its citizens, which is the root definition of terrorism.

While the U.S. has not yet devolved into full-blown Tyranny, we have entered its beginning steps. Elements of authoritarianism have entered daily government usage and are increasing exponentially. Edward Snowden's revelations of mass surveillance showcase how the government, in the name of protecting its citizens, wields its power in ways that infringe upon natural rights. The militarization of police forces, coupled with the suppression of protests and freedom of speech, further reflects the encroachment of Tyranny. I am not saying that protesters don't violate the rights of the innocent in some circumstances. Still, when analyzed and researched deeply, those actions are typically driven by the government and its agents pretending to be "protesting" against government oppression and authority. Plato's critique of

Democracy and its cyclical transition into Tyranny should be relevant to all of us. The U.S., like ancient Athens, has demonstrated how progressive freedom, economic inequality, and charismatic rulership can destabilize systems, paving the way for authoritarianism and a new Age of Tyranny.

Revolution: Reset

Revolution is the natural response to Tyranny, which restores justice and freedom. Revolutions are driven by the desire to replace oppressive systems with more reasonable forms of governance. However, despite the ideals presented as justification, revolutions result in a return to earlier forms of statism, perpetuating cycles of governance that align with Plato's observations on the lifecycle of government. Plato's theory posits that all political regimes, whether Aristocracy, Timocracy, Oligarchy, or Democracy, inevitably degenerate into Tyranny, thus leading back to the oppressive system they sought to overthrow. This cyclical nature of revolutions stresses the futility of repeating the same actions and expecting different results.

Revolutions are driven by the belief that a new system will resolve the failings of the old, which can bring about temporary change but reintroduce similar hierarchies and power structures. This cycle perpetuates the same issues under different pretenses, showing that revolutions only achieve temporary meaningful progress and mask the systemic inherent flaws in government. There is always potential for meaningful progress, but the repetitive nature of the government's revolution reflects the idiom of the definition of insanity -*doing the same thing repeatedly, expecting different results*. Humanity's inability to escape this cycle suggests deeper, systemic issues embedded within the human psyche and the need to be controlled.

Human psychology plays a significant role in perpetuating this endless cycle of Tyranny. Societies are conditioned to seek authority

Lifecycle of Government

figures for security and stability, which creates a dependency on the government. This dependency ensures that revolutions replace one set of rulers with another rather than addressing the deeper issues of authority and control. Understanding this psychological aspect is crucial to breaking free from Tyranny and emphasizes the need for systemic change.

The Chinese Dynastic Cycle illustrates how periods of unity and prosperity are inevitably followed by decline, rebellion, and the rise of a new dynasty. Similarly, Europe's oscillation between monarchy, republics, and dictatorships demonstrates the difficulty of breaking free from entrenched governance patterns and control. History is full of examples that show the lifecycle of government and provide compelling evidence for the argument that the belief in government is a fallacious idea. Remember, Plato, thousands of years ago, identified this endless cycle of tyrannical behavior using hundreds of years, if not longer, of political changes as evidence for his analytical findings.

Breaking the Cycle

Escaping the cyclical insanity of the need for government requires rethinking humanity's relationship with power, authority, and control. Rather than reacting to Tyranny with revolution, society must develop new paradigms prioritizing decentralization, natural rights, voluntarism, and innovation and evolve past the need to be controlled. Decentralizing power from centralized governments to localized, community-based facilitating systems can reduce corruption and enhance accountability, providing a path to absolute freedom.

Shifting from controlling entities to voluntary associations and exchanges encourages genuine collaboration and promises to reduce the potential for systemic abuse significantly. Promoting critical thinking through the Trivium and historical awareness equips us to recognize and resist manipulative rulers and tyranny and find alternate solutions to government. Anarchism is an alternative approach to government-run societies that focuses on mutual aid -voluntary associations and exchanges-, natural rights, and consensus-based decision-making and problem-solving, which will be discussed in detail in the last chapter of this book. Emerging technologies like blockchain and decentralized networks are more than just tools. They are disruptive forces and systems that can facilitate transparent strategic planning without reliance on centralized control. These Facilitating Systems can help free and organized communities function and operate with other communities.

Plato's analysis of government's lifecycle remains profoundly relevant today, highlighting the transition from earlier forms of statism to Tyranny and the cyclical nature of revolutions, emphasizing humanity's failure to address the flaws of governance and human behavior. Revolutions act as reset buttons, failing to break free from the repetitive patterns of the lifecycle of government Plato described. Breaking this cycle requires a paradigm shift -a move from centralized power and reactive revolutions toward decentralized, voluntary, and sustainable facilitating systems based on natural rights. By promoting voluntary collaboration and exchange, leveraging education and technology, and addressing the root causes of society's failures, humanity can evolve beyond statism and create a culture where natural rights, justice, and progress become enduring realities rather than fleeting ideals.

"*A government big enough to give you everything you want is a government big enough to take from you everything you have.*" – President Gerald R. Ford, *Presidential address to a joint session of Congress* (August 12th, 1974)

Protect and Serve: Reality

"The deterioration in police conduct, and the militarization of local police forces, quite simply and quite predictably mirrors the rise of the total state itself. We know that state monopolies invariably provide worse and worse services for more and more money. Police services are no exception. When it comes to your local police, there is no shopping around, there is no customer service, and there is no choice. Without market competition, market price signals, and market discipline, government has no ability or incentive to provide what people really want, which is peaceful and effective security for themselves, their families, their homes, and their property. As with everything government purports to provide, the public wants Andy Griffith but ends up with the Terminator." – Jeff Deist, *Police States and Private Markets* (August 23rd, 2014)

The phrase "**to protect and serve**" is widely recognized as a motto of law enforcement agencies across the U.S., embodying the idealized vision of police as more than just officers but as guardians of public safety and defenders of justice. However, the practical application of police reveals significant inconsistencies. It raises critical ethical and moral questions about the duties and responsibilities of police and the various law enforcement agencies in modern society. **Does the government protect and serve?**

The militarization of police forces, driven by policy decisions and cultural changes, has shifted the focus from community-oriented policing and protection to engaging in strategies that prioritize control, compliance, and force. This combative transformation not only weakens the confidence between law enforcement and the communities they supposedly serve but also poses serious threats to individual rights, creating conditions that lead to Tyranny.

Case Law: The Myth

The belief that police are legally obligated to protect and serve citizens is a common yet profoundly flawed misconception. While the motto "protect and serve" suggests a commitment to public safety, several landmark court cases have clarified that police and the government have no general duty to protect individuals. These rulings challenge the rhetoric of the police's role in public protection.

One pivotal case, ***Riss v. City of New York*, 240 N.E.2d 860 (N.Y. 1968)**, sets the legal precedent that government entities, including law enforcement, have no specific obligation to protect individuals. In this case, Linda Riss sought police protection after being threatened by a rejected suitor who later hired someone to throw lye in her face, leaving her permanently disfigured and partially blinded. Despite Riss's repeated pleas for help, the police failed to act preemptively to protect her. The court ruled that the police and the City of New York could not be held liable for failing to provide protection. The court's decision was based on law enforcement's duty to the public, not specific individuals. This ruling framed the limitations of relying on law enforcement for personal protection and revealed a gap between public perception of police duties and their legal obligations.

Another case is ***Warren v. District of Columbia*, 444 A.2d 1 (D.C. Ct. of App. 1981)**, in which three women were brutally attacked despite making multiple desperate calls to the police for help. The court ruled that the police owed no specific duty to protect the victims, expanding the legal precedent that law enforcement's responsibility is to the public, not individual citizens.

Similarly, ***DeShaney v. Winnebago County Department of Social Services*, 489 U.S. 189 (1989)** reinforced this principle. A four-year-old boy suffered severe and repeated abuse at the hands of his father despite prior reports to social services. The Supreme Court held that the state had no constitutional obligation to protect the child from private violence. This ruling emphasized that government agents, including police officers, are not required to intervene in individual harm unless a custodial relationship exists, e.g., criminals.

Another critical case, *Castle Rock v. Gonzales*, 545 U.S. 748 (2005), further solidified this legal precedent. In this case, a mother obtained a restraining order against her abusive husband, which was ultimately ignored by the police. Tragically, her three children were murdered by her estranged husband. The Supreme Court ruled that enforcing a restraining order is not mandatory, confirming that law enforcement is not obligated to protect individual citizens even in life-threatening situations.

These cases collectively expose a troubling legal reality: law enforcement agencies and the government are not legally bound to provide protection or assistance to individual citizens. This should call into question law enforcement's actual role and accountability in society. **Why would the government keep providing things it doesn't have to? Could it be a psychological way to manipulate control?** Remember, if the government can give it, it can take it away.

Role of Police Enforcement Officers

To understand the contemporary role of police, it's crucial to delve into the origins and evolution of the terms that define their function. The term **'police'** has its roots in the Greek *polis*, which refers to a "city-state," and the Latin *politia*, which means "civil administration." In essence, police share the same meaning as **'policy,'** a "way of management." This etymology reflects the historical role of policing and managing the policies and regulations necessary for maintaining order and control within a city-state. The term **'enforcement,'** derived from the Latin *enforcēre*, means "constraint or compulsion" through the use of "force, violence, rape, and oppression," underscoring the active role of police in ensuring compliance with laws and policies. The term '**officer**,' from the Latin *officium*, conveys the notion of duty or service, suggesting a professional obligation tied to the government's directives.

These elements collectively define a police enforcement officer as an agent of the government, primarily tasked with compelling adherence to laws, policies, and regulations through the use of force, violence, oppression, and, if necessary or desired, rape. This role positions them as instruments of authority, focusing on maintaining government-imposed order rather than protecting individual rights and freedoms. This contrasts with the idealized heroic phrase of "protecting and serving," as one might find with a true peacekeeper -someone dedicated to protecting tranquility and resolving general disputes without violence, coercion, or force; to protect and serve the innocent, not government rulers and their dictations.

In modern times, the role of the police has shifted dramatically from the envisioned role of peacekeepers to one of population management and control used to stifle dissent and disobedience. This transformation is evident in the militarization of police and the prioritization of government interests over individual rights. Modern police forces now embody the coercive arm of government authority and oppression, enforcing the policies of the ruling body while sidelining broader ideals of justice and peace. A term that more accurately describes their function today is "**policy enforcers**" -individuals who are primarily tasked with enforcing the policies and regulations of the government rather than maintaining peace while protecting natural rights. It is essential to recognize that this dynamic stems from the nature of the job, shaping the person's actions while performing their role within the system. The job is the issue; it is not always the individual, but always the individual when at the job.

Police Militarization

The evolution of police into militarized institutions, characterized by the adoption of military-grade equipment, tactics, and training, has deep historical roots. This departure from traditional community-oriented peacekeeping carries profound implications for natural rights. The militarization of police gained momentum with the introduction of the 1033 Program in 1990 under President George H. W. Bush's administration and expanded under President Bill Clinton's administration in 1997. This initiative allowed the Department of Defense to transfer surplus military equipment, such as armored vehicles, assault rifles, riot gear, and grenade launchers, to local law enforcement agencies. Intended initially to bolster police capabilities for drug enforcement, the program quickly expanded, equipping even small-town police departments with weaponry designed for combat zones.

The largest crime bill in U.S. history is the Violent Crime Control and Law Enforcement Act (VCCLEA) of 1994, proposed by then-Senator Joseph Biden of Delaware -now president- and signed into law by President Clinton. This Act comprised 356 pages of regulations and policies around what the government deemed as crimes and punishments and oversaw the training of 100 thousand new police officers. Since the creation of this Act, there has been a direct correlation to the rise of crime based on the Act, and it led to mass incarceration, racial disparities, mandatory minimum sentences, and a lack of community-based prevention and initiatives. Disrupting the home by sending individuals to prison for victimless crimes, such as drug use, further damaged entire generations growing up in "broken homes," leading to the public crises we see today. This is similar to the Global War on Terrorism (GWOT) that took place after the 9/11 attacks and how it bred more terrorism throughout the world, officially called "blowback."

The post-9/11 focus on counterterrorism further intensified this upward trend, with increased funding for paramilitary training and integrating battlefield tactics into urban policing. Police began adopting a mindset to combat perceived threats and crimes rather than foster community relations through protection and service. President Barack Obama limited the 1033 program through Executive Order 13688 in 2015, which was rolled back and eliminated by President Donald Trump in 2017.

Police militarization is not unique to the U.S.; it is a global phenomenon. In authoritarian regimes like China and Russia, heavily armed police units are regularly deployed to suppress dissent and disobedience and enforce strict governmental controls. For example, during the protests in Hong Kong, riot police used advanced weaponry, tear gas, and water cannons to disperse pro-democracy demonstrators, reinforcing the government's dominance and control. Police militarization is justified under the appearance of national security or crime prevention. This global trend raises significant concerns about the establishment of tyranny and violation of natural rights as the governments of the world quickly progress toward Tyranny.

Path Toward Tyranny

The militarization of police represents a larger pattern of government oppression, where government systems evolve to enforce authority at the expense of individual rights. Through the examination of case law and analysis of definitions, it becomes evident how militarized law enforcement serves as a tool of Tyranny, reinforcing authoritarian control and undermining individual rights and principles.

History provides us with numerous cautionary tales of militarized police being used to suppress dissent and consolidate power. As an example, the Praetorian Guard, established to protect the emperor during the decline of the Roman Republic, over time, it morphed into a force that upheld imperial rule and quashed any opposition, wielding significant political influence. Similarly, in Nazi Germany, the Gestapo, a militarized police force, used fear, violence, and surveillance to enforce government policies. Their operations systematically dismantled opposition and maintained the Nazi regime's stranglehold on power, illustrating the dangers of militarized policing as a tool of Tyranny.

One of the most concerning aspects of the militarization of police is the disappearance of accountability. Militarized police frequently operate with impunity, shielded by legal protections and limited oversight, e.g., police tend to be granted qualified immunity, giving them blanket immunity at the discretion of the level of violence they put forward in any given situation. However, the public's perception and acceptance of this lack of accountability perpetuates a culture where abuses of power are normalized, and violations of individual rights usually go unpunished. The resulting environment not only continues to shatter confidence but also solidifies the perception of police as enforcers of authority rather than protectors of rights, further bringing the government toward Tyranny.

The "**thin blue line**" motto, touted as a symbol of law enforcement solidarity, is a phrase that refers to the idea that police officers are the "thin blue line" that stands between order and chaos. However, critically analyzing the motto can drive the interpretation that mirrors gang-like behavior. This solidarity shields misconduct within the police, creating an "us versus them" mentality where officers protect other officers without caring about what is ethically and morally acceptable. Officers who attempt to expose corruption or excessive force often face ostracism or retaliation, much like individuals who defy gang loyalty. The unwritten code of silence that discourages officers from reporting wrongdoing parallels the practices of criminal organizations, emphasizing loyalty to the group over ethical behavior or accountability to the public.

Christopher Dorner is a prime example of ostracism and retaliation that can cause extreme situations. In February 2013, former officer Dorner began a killing spree targeting officers or their families for grievances over targeted racism and wrongful termination, which he said happened after he spoke out against fellow officers who he claimed to have committed excessive violence and force against suspects. The perceived retaliation by the police department drove Dorner to murder -his only believed recourse for seeing justice served.

As militarized police forces grow in strength and influence, their role evolves from protectors of "public safety and service" to enforcers of government tyranny, a police state. The use of advanced technology, such as military-grade equipment and surveillance tactics, in civilian settings escalates tensions, especially during protests or demonstrations. Instead of cultivating dialogue and resolution, these displays of force intimidate citizens and suppress opposition and freedom of speech. Over time, this dynamic creates an environment where fear replaces faith, and compliance is demanded rather than earned. It can be argued that we have been in this environment for years.

Surveillance, curfews, and the suppression of assembly are implemented under the premise of needed security, further concentrating authority. In some cases, martial law is enacted to oppress further and restrict those who might be defiant. Martial law is a state of direct military control over civilian populations, usually in response to a temporary emergency such as an invasion or major disaster. It involves curfews, suspending civil law, and using military force to maintain order and stifle disobedience. Marginalized communities usually bear the brunt of this repression, deepening social divisions and exacerbating public discontent and strife.

As history shows, unchecked militarization and the attrition of freedoms and rights eventually push societies toward a breaking point. The combination of systemic oppression, economic inequality, and the silencing of dissent fuels resentment and desperation among the masses. Revolution through disobedience becomes an almost inevitable

Protect and Serve: Reality

response when avenues for peaceful redress are blocked. The French Revolution, the fall of the Roman Republic, and the uprisings in colonial America all illustrate how authoritarian overreach can and will ignite movements to reclaim freedom and justice. However, these revolutions reset the cycle rather than breaking it, and it is never a peaceful event due to tyranny's willingness to commit violence to maintain control. The power vacuum left by overthrowing a tyrannical system is frequently filled by new regimes that replicate the same patterns of control and suppression.

By its very nature, the government is an institution of control designed to enforce compliance, consolidate authority, and maintain power. This inherent purpose makes it predisposed to evolve into Tyranny. The belief that the government exists to serve and protect individual rights and citizens is a dangerous misconception -a fallacy that perpetuates its expansion and overreach. We must be acutely aware of and cautious about this misconception. We have the power to challenge it.

The progression of militarized police illustrates the trajectory toward Tyranny. Law enforcement, initially touted as an institution meant to "protect and serve," has evolved into a powerful arm of government control, equipped with military-grade tools and operating with increasing impunity. This shift provides a chilling reality: there is no law too small that the government won't enforce, even to the point of lethal force, a fact that should shock and concern everyone. This transformation reveals a disturbing prioritization of authority and compliance over justice and public service principles.

Legal precedents have further entrenched this reality by absolving police and government of any obligation to protect individual citizens, revealing their role as enforcers of government power rather than guardians of public safety. This shift is not an aberration but an extension of the very nature of government. The systemic militarization of police corresponding to the reduction of individual rights brings into focus the inherent flaws in the belief that the government can be reformed to maintain the principles of justice and natural rights. Efforts to address authoritarian governance through incremental reforms must recognize that the root issue lies in the government itself. Its structure and purpose inherently push those under its control toward Tyranny, making the cycle of unrest and revolution an inevitability. Each iteration of this cycle replaces one form of centralized authority with another, perpetuating the same systemic issues under a different name with the same fallacious belief that this time will be better.

"No man has greater regard for the military gentlemen than I have. I admire their intrepidity, perseverance, and valour. But when once a standing army is established, in any country, the people lose their liberty. When against a regular and disciplined army, yeomanry are the only defense — yeomanry, unskillful & unarmed, what chance is there for preserving freedom?" – George Mason, *Addresses to the Virginia Ratifying Convention* (June 14th, 1788)

Constitutional Contradictions

"The constitution, on this hypothesis, is a mere thing of wax in the hands of the judiciary, which they may twist and shape into any form they please." – Thomas Jefferson, *letter to Judge Spencer Roane* (September 6th, 1819); reported in Andrew A. Lipscomb, ed., *The Writings of Thomas Jefferson* (1904)

The U.S. Constitution is hailed as an essential aspect of U.S. culture and is celebrated for protecting individual rights and defining the federal government's power limitations. Each state in the U.S. also has state constitutions that outline how that state government should function. The Constitution does not bestow or outline natural rights and individual freedoms. Instead, it is a framework crafted to curb the government's power, ensuring that its authority does not infringe upon the inherent rights of the people. Any item not explicitly defined in the Constitution is left up to each state to decide. Despite these idealized intentions, the historical and contemporary applications of the Constitution reveal systemic contradictions that challenge its effectiveness as a defender of rights and citizens.

While natural rights are inherent to all individuals, the Constitution was not the source of these rights. It was, however, written with the idealization that the role of government is not to bestow these rights but to protect them. This paradox challenges the claim that the government is here for our protection and service. The government views that it only has to provide protection and services to those physically under its care, criminals, so **why should we have faith in the government to protect and serve us while also abiding by the limitations set in the Constitution?**

Constitutional Contradictions

The founders and framers of the U.S. intended to construct a system that imposed strict limits on governmental power and provided avenues for citizens to protect themselves. The Constitution's purpose, therefore, was to serve as a restraint on authority, delineating what the government could and could not do. However, the effectiveness of these restraints has been consistently subverted by the institution they were designed to limit, posing serious questions about the efficacy of stopping the government from evolving into Tyranny.

Over time, the Constitution's role as a check on government power has been thwarted through deliberate reinterpretation or neglect. While its language sets clear boundaries, history shows that these boundaries are frequently attacked in the name of public interest, crisis management, evolving social needs, or sophistry by those who intend to misuse government for increased power. This flexibility, while sometimes hailed as a feature of a "living document," also paves the way for systemic overreach, weakening its role as a protector against oppression and tyrannical rule.

The contradictions between the Constitution's purpose and application become particularly evident when examining how it has been used to justify expansions of power. From the suspension of *habeas corpus* -the court's demand for a detailed person to be brought before the court- during the Civil War to the proliferation of executive orders in modern administrations, the flexibility of constitutional interpretation has been leveraged to bypass its intended limitations. While frequently framed as necessary for the greater good, these actions are a persistent tension between the Constitution's theoretical purpose and the realities of practical applications.

The Constitution's reliance on the vigilance of the uninformed governed presents a potential flaw. It presupposes an active, informed populace capable of holding government accountable to its limitations. When this vigilance fades, the balance shifts, allowing the government to operate beyond its intended scope. This shift toward Tyranny is not just a failure of those in power but a direct challenge to the

Constitution's capacity to protect individual rights. It is also a glaring example of the government's constant progress toward Tyranny.

The following list only covers some of the Constitutional Amendments and is not a complete list:

First Amendment: Government Censorship

Congress shall make no law respecting an establishment of religion, or prohibiting the free exercise thereof; or abridging the freedom of speech, or of the press; or the right of the people peaceably to assemble, and to petition the Government for a redress of grievances.

The First Amendment guarantees the Right to Freedom of Speech. However, government actions have purposely limited this fundamental right, especially within social media platforms. As platforms like X (formerly Twitter), Instagram, Facebook, and YouTube have evolved into the modern public square, they have also become focal points for censorship and the suppression of dissenting views against approved government rhetoric. This alarming trend raises concerns about how constitutional protections are being circumvented in the digital age.

Government agencies have increasingly collaborated with and demanded social media platforms to regulate and suppress identified content, justifying their actions as efforts to combat misinformation or extremism. The Twitter Files, a series of internal documents released in 2022, revealed how agencies like the Federal Bureau of Investigation (FBI) and the Department of Homeland Security (DHS) pressured Twitter to remove posts and accounts that challenged the prevailing rhetoric during the COVID19 pandemic. This influence and dictation blurred the line between the public and private sectors, with the government using these platforms to silence voices and opposition deemed problematic and disobedient.

Whistleblowers have provided crucial testimony to congressional committees about the depth of these collaborations. They have exposed how government-funded initiatives have targeted political speech under the appearance of national security or public health. This strategy not only suppresses dissent but also creates a chilling effect, discouraging individuals from expressing views that deviate from the mainstream or face de-platforming bans and suspensions.

In *State of Missouri v. Biden*, No. 22-40526 (5th Cir. 2023), the court found that federal agencies likely violated the First Amendment by coercing social media platforms into censoring content. This case is significant as it sheds light on how the government's involvement in regulating digital speech infringes upon constitutional protections.

Another example is the de-platforming of the popular social media platform Parler among conservative users. Following the "insurrection" of January 6th, 2021, Amazon Web Services (AWS) terminated Parler's hosting services, effectively shutting it down. This action and Apple and Google's decisions to remove Parler from their app stores demonstrated a trend of collusion between corporations and the government to suppress specific political viewpoints. This serves as a reminder of the government's power over digital speech and its threat to our freedom of speech.

Second Amendment: Arms Ownership and Tyranny

A well regulated Militia, being necessary to the security of a free State, the right of the people to keep and bear Arms, shall not be infringed.

The Second Amendment was designed not only to protect individual self-defense but also to serve as a broader safeguard against the potential overreach of that very government, ensuring that the people retained the ability to resist tyranny and uphold their freedoms. The phrase "**bear arms**" historically referred to military service and carrying weapons in military combat. However, the use of '**Arms**' with a capital 'A' broadens this protection to include all weapons and tools of war that a government could use against its citizens. This linguistic distinction is vital for understanding the founders' recognition of the need for citizens to remain armed and to have the ability and the right to defend against an oppressive government.

The symbolic significance of Arms is further reflected in the "**coat of arms**" of the U.S. -the flag- which represents the nation and its government. This symbol is prominently displayed on the shoulders of soldiers who go into battle, signifying their allegiance to the government. Many fail to recognize the intrinsic connection between the flag and the government it represents. History demonstrates that when a government is overthrown during a revolution, a new coat of arms -a flag- is established, symbolizing the shift in power and governance. This intrinsic link reveals that supporting and defending the flag inherently supports and defends the government it embodies.

The interpretation and enforcement of this protected right have sparked heated debates and controversies. Questions surrounding the scope of "Arms" and the balance between public safety and individual rights have fueled ongoing tensions. Nonetheless, the core intent of the Second Amendment remains clear: to serve as a critical check against tyranny and to preserve the ability of citizens to defend their rights against any force that threatens to undermine them.

A prominent example is the Battle of Athens in 1946, where armed citizens in Tennessee took up arms to overthrow corrupt local officials who were manipulating elections. This event exemplifies how the founders' intent for an armed populace was to maintain a balance of power and prevent government tyranny. As seen today, this type of behavior is considered domestic terrorism by the government.

The Second Amendment faces increasing challenges through various gun control measures, which are always under the pretext of public safety. Policies such as assault weapon bans and magazine restrictions infringe on the rights of the innocent. For example,

President Trump violated the Second Amendment when he enacted a bump stock ban in 2018, which was overturned by the Supreme Court in 2024 as unconstitutional. President Trump enacted more gun control during his first term than President Obama throughout his two terms. Yet, President Trump's supporters staunchly claim he is pro-Second Amendment and a defender of our rights. This contrasts with President Trump's view of "take guns first, go through due process second." Additionally, states like California and Washington, with their strict gun laws -among the most restrictive in the U.S.- disarm innocent and responsible gun owners while failing to address violent crime rates as promised.

Red Flag laws allow authorities to confiscate firearms and weapons without due process from individuals deemed a risk. This risk is entirely subjective based on the government's views and opinions. A striking example occurred in Maryland in 2018 when a 61-year-old man was unjustly killed during the enforcement of a Red Flag law, raising concerns about violations of individual rights and the potential for misuse. The police were notified by the man's sister, who was worried that he might be potentially suicidal. Her actions and law enforcement's aggressive use of force and violence to end situations led to an innocent man's murder.

The gradual attrition of Second Amendment protections reflects a troubling trend of disempowering individuals while strengthening the government's monopoly on violence and force. This shift sabotages the founders' intent and raises critical questions about the balance of power between citizens and their government.

In August 2016, I wrote an article on *What made America great?*. During this research, I tried to determine what truly made America great. I concluded that only the founders' defiance in the face of tyranny made America great. This led me to develop the phrase "**Make America Defiant Again**" and design the following image, highlighting this once-great act and its implications.

Constitutional Contradictions

Fourth Amendment: Privacy Violations

The right of the people to be secure in their persons, houses, papers, and effects, against unreasonable searches and seizures, shall not be violated, and no Warrants shall issue, but upon probable cause, supported by Oath or affirmation, and particularly describing the place to be searched, and the persons or things to be seized.

The Fourth Amendment was established to protect citizens from unreasonable searches and seizures. However, it has become increasingly undermined by pervasive and systemic practices in law enforcement and government surveillance. The violation of privacy -a fundamental right- remains widespread despite the constitutional protections promised, raising serious concerns about individual rights.

One significant area of concern is police overreach with policies like New York City's controversial Stop-and-Frisk program, which disproportionately targeted minority communities and is typically used without probable cause. These practices not only violated Fourth Amendment rights but also perpetuated systemic inequalities. Similarly, civil asset forfeiture, where law enforcement agencies seize property from individuals without proving a crime occurred, violates the Amendment's intent. We must remember that without a victim, there is no crime.

Mass surveillance programs represent another violation of the Fourth Amendment. Whistleblower Edward Snowden played a pivotal role in exposing the National Security Agency's (NSA) extensive data collection initiatives, such as PRISM, which spied on citizens without obtaining warrants. These programs are part of a surveillance state ignoring the Right to Privacy. The indiscriminate collection of phone records, emails, and other personal data showcases how technological advancements have been weaponized against the liberties the Fourth Amendment sought to protect. These violations paint a grim picture of how the Fourth Amendment has been ignored and sidelined.

Fifth Amendment: Due Process

No person shall be held to answer for a capital, or otherwise infamous crime, unless on a presentment or indictment of a Grand Jury, except in cases arising in the land or naval forces, or in the Militia, when in actual service in time of War or public danger; nor shall any person be subject for the same offence to be twice put in jeopardy of life or limb; nor shall be compelled in any criminal case to be a witness against himself, nor be deprived of life, liberty, or property, without due process of law; nor shall private property be taken for public use, without just compensation.

The Fifth Amendment was created to protect due process, a cornerstone of justice that should ensure no person can be deprived of life, freedom, or property without fair procedures. Despite this guarantee, government actions impede these protections, revealing a troubling trend of disregarding constitutional safeguards.

One glaring example occurred in 2018 when President Trump suggested, "**Take the guns first, go through due process second**," during discussions on Red Flag laws. This statement reflects a dangerous precedent of prioritizing expediency over constitutional protections. Such measures directly conflict with the Second Amendment and Fifth Amendment's requirement for due process before depriving individuals of their property.

Federal and state governments' widespread use of civil asset forfeiture further exemplifies this disregard for due process. Under this practice, law enforcement agencies seize property suspected of being connected to criminal activity, usually without formal charges or trials. Victims are left to navigate complex legal systems to reclaim their assets, a burden that disproportionately affects marginalized and lower-income individuals.

These examples show the limitations of the Fifth Amendment and how the government can circumvent constitutional protections, especially when it prioritizes efficiency and control over individual rights. Without steadfast adherence to due process, attacks on rights become the norm rather than an exception, further advancing the government toward Tyranny.

Ninth Amendment: Beyond the Constitution

The enumeration in the Constitution, of certain rights, shall not be construed to deny or disparage others retained by the people.

The philosophical foundation of the Ninth Amendment, as articulated by thinkers like John Locke, acknowledges that the rights identified in the Constitution are not exhaustive, emphasizing that inherent and natural rights exist independently of government recognition. This principle aims to limit governmental overreach by setting the expectation that a piece of paper does not define rights. Locke argued that all individuals are inherently entitled to rights such as life, liberty (freedom), and property, which governments must respect and protect. However, the Constitution's inability to prevent encroachments on natural rights shows its limitations, which are often overlooked, leading to significant challenges in protecting unenumerated rights.

One of the most glaring examples of ignoring the Ninth Amendment's intent is the federal government's trend toward overcriminalization. By continuously expanding the scope of laws and regulations across all industries, the government not only infringes on individual rights but also threatens the very fabric of society. These actions show a troubling pattern where the government intervenes in areas that should be addressed through personal autonomy rather than legal mandates.

The sheer volume of federal laws and regulations in the U.S. shows the legal system's complexity and ever-expanding nature. Since 1789, Congress has enacted thousands of statutes, with each session contributing between 200 and 600 new laws, culminating in an estimated total of over 30,000 statutes. These laws are organized into the U.S. Code, consolidating general and permanent statutes into 54 subject-specific titles, excluding temporary or situational ones.

Complementing these statutes are federal regulations compiled in the Code of Federal Regulations (CFR), which consists of 50 titles detailing the implementation of laws. Between 1995 and 2016 alone, nearly 89,000 federal regulations were issued compared to 4,312 laws enacted by Congress, illustrating the disproportionate growth of regulatory rules and control. The dynamic nature of this system, with constant updates, amendments, and repeals, makes quantifying the exact number of laws and regulations nearly impossible, leaving a vast and ever-evolving legal infrastructure of unknown proportions. Even though this enormous and cumbersome legal behemoth exists, the government expects us to be intimately aware of all the laws and regulations and how we should interact concerning them. This expectation doesn't apply to the government and its agents due to the qualified immunity that the government applies to itself.

Thirteenth Amendment: Legalized Slavery

Neither slavery nor involuntary servitude, except as a punishment for crime whereof the party shall have been duly convicted, shall exist within the United States, or any place subject to their jurisdiction.

The Thirteenth Amendment is celebrated for abolishing slavery; however, it contains a significant loophole: it permits forced labor, slavery, and involuntary servitude as punishment for a crime. This exception has effectively legalized slavery, making it a constitutionally protected action within the penal system, particularly in private prisons, where profit is derived from inmate labor. With over 2 million incarcerated individuals, the U.S. holds the largest prison population globally, and many inmates are forced to work for rates as low as 23 cents per hour. Private prison corporations, such as CoreCivic and GEO Group, capitalize on this system, turning imprisonment into a lucrative industry.

An example of the dangerous precedent and warning of how power corrupts is the case of Michael Conahan, a former judge who became a convicted felon in 2008 after accepting $2.8 million for jailing more than 3,200 children to privately run detention centers in a "kids for cash" scheme. Conahan was sentenced to 17.5 years in prison but was released from prison and rendered to home confinement in 2020 due to COVID19 concerns. Before leaving office in December 2024, President Biden commuted the rest of Conahan's sentence to the displeasure of the victims and their families.

Far from eradicating the institution of slavery, the amendment merely limits its scope, allowing the government to control and exploit a new form of coerced labor in the name of criminal justice. The language of the Thirteenth Amendment permits slavery for those "duly convicted" of a crime, which raises ethical questions about how crimes are defined and enforced by the government. **No victim, no crime.** The criminalization of minor infractions and victimless crimes, such as jaywalking, disproportionately impacts minorities, perpetuating systemic racism within the justice system.

In states like Louisiana, where incarceration rates are among the highest in the nation, inmate labor is heavily relied upon for public works, further entrenching modern slavery. Roughly 20% of the world's prison population resides in the U.S., with minorities overrepresented in these numbers. This reflects a broader pattern where government policies and law enforcement practices selectively target minority communities, perpetuating racial and economic inequality through legalized slavery.

Individuals are not and should never be considered property. The concept of '**property**' is a natural inherent right that is found within all individuals. Slavery is an immoral, unethical, and evil practice, and any document intended to protect individual rights that permits slavery must be regarded as fundamentally flawed and a poor litmus test for justice. The presence of a loophole allowing slavery directly contradicts the principles of natural rights and equality that such a document purports to defend. A genuine protector of rights would unequivocally eliminate any avenue for exploitation or systemic oppression.

Sixteenth Amendment: Income Tax

The Congress shall have power to lay and collect taxes on incomes, from whatever source derived, without apportionment among the several States, and without regard to any census or enumeration.

Constitutional Contradictions

Ratified in 1913, the Sixteenth Amendment granted Congress the authority to impose income taxes, altering the relationship between individuals and the federal government. Before the ratification, income taxes were deemed unconstitutional through the court case *Pollock v. Farmers' Loan & Trust Company*, **157 U.S. 429 (1895)**. This change centralized economic power, enabling the government to control personal wealth and channel it toward its priorities. To make matters worse, as of 2025, a substantial portion of federal tax revenue is allocated to making payments toward the national debt rather than funding public services, stressing the disconnect between taxpayer contributions and social benefits. For example, military spending and interest payments on debt overshadow investments in education, infrastructure, or healthcare by a significant amount, raising questions about the ethical justification for such forced contributions.

The introduction of the Sixteenth Amendment in 1913 was closely tied to creating the Federal Reserve System through the Federal Reserve Act of 1913. The *Panic of 1907* -a financial crisis fueled by speculation and propaganda- helped drive the support for the act. In 1907, trust in financial institutions like the Knickerbocker Trust Company significantly dropped after a failed attempt by its president, Charles T. Barney, to corner the copper stock market, leading to a bank run when the scheme failed, and the stock plummeted. The New York Times - recently purchased with the backing of J. P. Morgan- amplified public fear through sophist rhetoric, creating the conditions for a bank run and manufactured economic turmoil. J. P. Morgan, a figure of immense influence, stepped in as a "savior," using his wealth and influence to stabilize the situation. To settle the issues, J. P. Morgan acquired assets like the Tennessee Coal, Iron, and Railroad Company (TCI) at fire sale prices, one of the largest users of prison labor -slave labor. This strategic maneuver eliminated a major competitor of U.S. Steel for J. P. Morgan and expanded his empire by exploiting convict labor.

John D. Rockefeller Jr. proposed creating a central bank to prevent future crises, an idea discussed at length during secretive meetings at

Jekyll Island. These meetings culminated in the Federal Reserve Act of 1913. The Federal Reserve -a consortium of private banks in coordination with the federal government- centralized monetary policy and concentrated power in the hands of a few, perpetuating the financial dominance of entities like J. P. Morgan and Rockefeller. The implementation of the Sixteenth Amendment around the same time ensured a steady revenue stream for the federal government to fund these centralized initiatives, creating a system of financial control that persists today.

Far from coincidental, these events reflect a calculated strategy by a few to reshape the economic landscape. The alignment of media, corporate, and governmental interests results in outcomes prioritizing control, setting a precedent for the systemic destruction of natural rights. The legacy of the Sixteenth Amendment emphasizes a troubling concentration of economic power in the hands of the government and financial elites. By controlling income and directing wealth toward questionable ends, this amendment has become a tool for systemic control and to keep people poor as they are more burdened than the elite, who can easily manage the limited taxes they are forced to pay by having the resources to find all legal loopholes reducing their tax burden.

While heralded as the foundation of governance and freedom, the U.S. Constitution has significant flaws and contradictions. Despite its promise to secure freedoms and protect individual rights, it permitted slavery through the Thirteenth Amendment's loophole, failing to uphold the principle of universal freedom. This oversight reflects a broader pattern where the Constitution has served as a tool for systemic violations of natural rights. Government overreach in censorship, taxation, and incarceration further illustrates how the document's ideals have been sabotaged and subverted to what some might consider a useless document.

Constitutional Contradictions

The Constitution is a set of guidelines written on paper and subject to interpretation, manipulation, and outright violation by the government and its agents. Governments frequently overstep the limits they impose without consequence, destroying their legitimacy as a blueprint for justice and morality. Despite being framed as a protector of individual rights, the U.S. Constitution has failed to prevent the government from inching toward Tyranny. While it has provided a starting point for recognizing natural rights, its limitations reveal how constitutions cannot be entrusted to keep governments in check. For a society to thrive and be free, it must go beyond a constitution's constraints and limitations and establish systems and principles prioritizing individual natural rights and moral integrity over government control. Society can only hope to build a model that genuinely protects and values natural rights and justice by addressing these structural deficiencies. Until this happens, the cyclical progression toward Tyranny will continue.

"The principles of a free constitution are irrecoverably lost, when the legislative power is nominated by the executive." – Edward Gibbon, *History of the Decline and Fall of the Roman Empire* (1838)

Education as a Tool of Indoctrination

"One of the painful signs of years of dumbed-down education is how many people are unable to make a coherent argument. They can vent their emotions, question other people's motives, make bold assertions, repeat slogans-- anything except reason." – Thomas Sowell, *Random Thoughts* (September 3rd, 2007)

Education is celebrated as a vital pathway to personal empowerment and enlightenment, feeding critical thinking and preparing individuals for active social participation and entry into the professional landscape of their chosen career. The U.S. education system is touted as the bastion of freedom, creativity, and independent thought. However, a closer examination and analysis reveals that it and many other educational systems, particularly in the modern era, have been deliberately structured to achieve the opposite: to control minds rather than free them.

Through their design and implementation, these systems prioritize conformity, obedience, and memorization over creativity, intellectual curiosity, and the cultivation of critical thinking. This is an essential reason why the Trivium is of such importance to be incorporated into our daily lives. We should question the true purpose of education and its role in shaping social structures, especially when made compulsory by the government. Questioning the government's stated educational intent and determining if it is true requires reevaluating our current educational system and aligning the results with the supposed principles of creativity and critical thought to see if they match.

Education as a Tool of Indoctrination

Throughout history, education has been a powerful tool, not for enlightenment but for indoctrination. Its evolution mirrors the priorities and values of those in power, perpetuating social hierarchies and stifling disobedience. This illustrates how the structure and content of education can foster independent growth or serve as a tool of control. At the heart of this analysis are three distinct educational paradigms: the Classical Trivium, the Prussian education system, and the fusion into the U.S. education system.

Classical Trivium: Literacy Slaves

The Classical Trivium, a system developed in ancient Greece and later adopted by the Catholic Church, played a significant role in education development. The Church used the Classical Trivium to create a systematic body of knowledge among learners, but only approved knowledge was provided. This selective approach was a means for the Church to keep followers within their approved body of knowledge while disciplining those who tried to go beyond that body of knowledge. The Classical Trivium, similar to the Trivium Method of Critical Thinking, consists of three sequential stages: Grammar, Logic, and Rhetoric. While this framework provided a foundation for structured learning, its application prioritized maintaining existing power structures through dictated knowledge over independent thought.

The Grammar stage focuses on approved knowledge, such as vocabulary, definitions, and basic concepts. While this stage is essential for understanding any subject, it was used to confine learners within predefined approved boundaries. For example, in the context of the Catholic Church, the Grammar stage established a rigid understanding of dogma. Questioning or stepping outside these boundaries was discouraged, limiting free inquiry, intellectual freedom, and independent thought. By controlling the foundational body of knowledge imparted, the Church ensured that learners' understanding aligned with its doctrinal teachings.

The Logic stage aimed to teach reasoning, but only within the constraints of the knowledge imparted during the Grammar stage. Instead of fostering open-ended questioning, this stage reinforced the internal consistency of the established dogma by using fallacious arguments as the only path forward. For example, medieval scholars were trained to reconcile and accept conflicting biblical interpretations rather than challenge the scriptures' validity. Logic was not a tool for exploring new ideas but a mechanism for solidifying and defending pre-existing belief structures.

The Rhetoric stage involved teaching students how to communicate their approved knowledge effectively. While it allegedly aimed to spark debate and discussion, this stage was frequently used to propagate established ideologies rather than encourage independent talks. Students were taught to defend the status quo, further entrenching ideas and concepts learned during the earlier stages of the Classical Trivium.

The Classical Trivium imposed significant limitations and sought to create what can be termed "literacy slaves" -individuals competent enough to work and labor but not competent enough to think for themselves. This was achieved by stifling critical thinking. By restricting free inquiry and aligning education with the priorities of power structures, the Classical Trivium ensured that knowledge served the interests of existing authorities rather than challenging them. Understanding these limitations is crucial for a critical and aware perspective on the educational system. In the U.S., the principles of the Classical Trivium have been integrated into modern education systems as a foundational structure. This integration maintains control over thought and behavior, perpetuating the same constraints on free thought that rulers and monarchs historically used to maintain control over their subjects.

Education as a Tool of Indoctrination

Prussian Education System: Blind Obedience

The Prussian education system, which emerged in the late 18th century as a response to Prussia's defeat by Napoleon, was a pivotal moment in the history of education. The Prussians, renowned for their military prowess and nation-building capabilities, attributed their defeat to soldiers' independent thinking. This conclusion fueled a compelling need to reform the education system, shaping it into a tool for indoctrinating students and society into blind obedience to authority. The system was designed to instill unquestioning loyalty among citizens and soldiers, crucial for maintaining power and avoiding further defeats. Schools were structured to prioritize memorization and the internalization of government-approved values, molding students into compliant members of society serving the government's interests.

The Prussian education system introduced several defining features that emphasized standardization and control. One of these was a federally approved standardized curriculum that left little room for regional or individual variation, ensuring all students received the same approved education. Another hallmark movement was the segregation of students into age-based peer brackets, reinforcing conformity by discouraging cross-age collaboration and exchanging diverse ideas, similar to elementary, middle, and high school segmentation by age. Centralized control of education was another critical feature, with teachers serving as government agents to ensure that the content and delivery of education aligned closely with government objectives.

The progression of Prussia into Nazi Germany is a demonstration of how the foundations of the Prussian education system laid the groundwork for an authoritarian regime. This system conditioned citizens to prioritize government authority over individual freedoms, suppressing independent thought and forcing a culture of compliance. As Prussia unified Germany in the late 19th century, these principles became central to the national identity. The rise of the Nazi Party capitalized on this legacy, leveraging a population accustomed to deference to authority and collective loyalty. Adolf Hitler and the Nazi regime extended and intensified these views, using propaganda, youth organizations like the Hitler Youth, and strict educational reforms to control the population further and eliminate dissent and disobedience. The result was a society primed to follow orders and accept totalitarian rule without question, illustrating the long-term consequences of an education system designed to produce obedient citizens rather than critical thinkers. This lasting impact on the society's culture and values is a crucial aspect to consider when evaluating the Prussian education system's legacy. The Prussian model has had a profound global influence, particularly in the U.S., where its principles were adopted to instill discipline and structure.

U.S. Education System: Modern Indoctrination

The U.S. education system is a fusion of the Classical Trivium and Prussian education system, significantly influencing social norms. The U.S. education system is compulsory, with laws adopted to regulate truancy -the illegal absence of mandatory education. The basis of the U.S. education system started with the Classical Trivium, which later adopted the Prussian education system. In the early to mid-19th century, Horace Mann, a leading education reformer, admired the Prussian education system and sought to implement its features across the U.S. Believing it would help create an "educated electorate" capable of sustaining a society, Mann began the establishment of compulsory education and a more standardized, accessible public education system.

However, the primary legacy of the Prussian model in the U.S. education system has been the suppression of individuality and creativity and blind obedience, which was the desired outcome. The system stifles innovation and perpetuates reverence for authority by prioritizing unquestioning compliance. The education system controls and indoctrinates by presenting only approved information and rhetoric.

Education as a Tool of Indoctrination

While many subjects are within the curricula, the practical implementation prioritizes conformity and compliance over intellectual growth. The system's influence is evident in how it teaches subjects like history, science, and literature, using rhetoric that reflects the priorities of dominant political or economic systems. Additionally, reciting the Pledge of Allegiance to the flag, government, and nation was established as a requirement to begin each school day to foster patriotism and unity in students and generations.

Another example of patriotic indoctrination can be seen at the beginning of professional sports matches, such as the National Football League's (NFL) displays of patriotism before games start. This display of patriotism is not an organic expression of national pride selflessly created by an organization but funded by local, state, and federal contracts. In 2015, it was revealed that the Department of Defense (DoD) paid the NFL millions of taxpayer dollars to promote patriotism and pro-military messages. This included scheduling pre-game flyovers, salutes to the troops, and patriotic shows. These displays foster a sense of nationalism and allegiance, reinforcing that supporting military actions and government policies is synonymous with patriotism. By associating these sentiments with a beloved pastime, the government leverages the appeal of emotion to influence public perception. This direct psychological tactic of manipulating feelings and thoughts shifts rhetoric from a place of critical thinking to blind obedience, fostering a belief and desire where loyalty to the government becomes intertwined with prideful identity and entertainment. **How do you react when you see someone "disrespect" U.S. patriotism or flag during a game?**

Primary education textbooks -produced by corporations and heavily influenced by the government- shape our past and present rhetoric within classrooms. This allows sophistry to alter terms, context, and themes, making the truth complicated to discern and confusing students at an early age. Textbooks present sanitized versions of history, omitting inconvenient truths such as systemic racism, which is frequently minimized or ignored in the curricula or hyper-focused as a way to breed hate against other citizens, as with Critical Race Theory or Diversity, Equity, and Inclusion. These efforts pushed by the government to "educate" always have ulterior motives beyond their stated goals. This control over information limits students' exposure to diverse perspectives and understanding of critical thinking as a skill set, contributing to perpetuating social norms and suppressing independent thought, leading society and government toward Tyranny.

Standardized testing remains central to U.S. education, emphasizing memorization and adherence to predetermined answers at the expense of creativity and understanding. This rigid system constrains teachers, who face professional repercussions if they challenge the status quo. It further suppresses independent thought in classrooms and institutes a system that rewards bad habits in the name of conformity. Standardized testing compounds this issue by rewarding conformity and penalizing creative or unconventional thinking, shifting educational priorities from critical thought to "teaching to the test."

Education has been a tool for propagating dominant ideologies and suppressing opposing perspectives throughout history. During the Cold War, U.S. schools actively promoted anti-communist sentiment, with textbooks glorifying capitalism and democracy while portraying communism as inherently evil. Programs like "duck and cover" drills normalized fear of nuclear war and reinforced the rhetoric of an ever-present external threat. In colonized nations, education systems were weaponized to erase indigenous cultures and instill the values of colonial powers. For example, residential schools in the U.S. stripped Indigenous children of their languages, traditions, and identities, causing long-lasting harm to their communities. Similarly, post-9/11 education in the U.S. emphasized patriotism and support for military actions abroad, equating dissent with disloyalty and stifling critical debate in preference for conformity. These examples demonstrate how government-approved education systems have historically served as instruments of ideological control, inflicting emotional and

Education as a Tool of Indoctrination

psychological harm on students rather than tools for independent thought.

Modern education significantly impacts social dynamics. It stifles the development of critical thinking skills, leaving individuals more susceptible to manipulation by political and corporate interests. The system's emphasis on workforce preparation ensures a steady supply of compliant workers while discouraging critical examination of systemic exploitation, such as the financial burden of student debt and the structures that perpetuate it. Additionally, this system advances social fragmentation and divisions by promoting dominant ideologies and disregarding dissenting perspectives.

To make matters worse, the government has increased school surveillance technologies, such as cameras and online monitoring software, normalizing constant oversight and conditioning students to accept invasive authority and having active police officers -school resource officers- turning some schools into prison-like establishments. Strict disciplinary policies, including zero-tolerance rules and regulations, disproportionately target marginalized communities, perpetuating systemic inequalities while instilling fear of non-conformity that further perpetuates systemic disparities. This environment creates and nurtures a direct pathway to the prison system.

The U.S. education system is a potent blend of the Classical Trivium and the Prussian education system. It has evolved into a tool that prioritizes conformity, suppresses critical thought, and rewards blind obedience to authority. This control-centric approach, emphasizing memorization, obedience, and workforce preparation, has ignored the nurturing of intellectual curiosity and independent thought and reasoning. Consequently, generations of students and citizens have been conditioned and indoctrinated to accept dominant mainstream government-approved rhetoric without question and defer to authority. This has reduced society's capacity to question systemic injustices and

Education as a Tool of Indoctrination

a growing oppressive, tyrannical government. The parallels between the U.S. education system and historical examples, such as Prussia's education reforms leading to Nazi Germany's indoctrination of youth, are apparent. They expose the dangers of education being weaponized for control rather than enlightenment. By preventing dissent and disobedience while promoting compliance, the U.S. education system plays a pivotal role in gradually destroying freedoms and rights, centralizing power, and driving the government toward Tyranny.

"There can be but one German Youth Movement, because there is but one way in which German youth can be educated and trained... This Reich stands, and is building itself up anew, upon its youth. And this Reich will hand over its youth to no one, but will take its education and its formation upon itself." – Adolf Hitler, *Public Speech* (May 1st, 1937)

Taxation is Theft

"Governments create nothing and have nothing to give but what they have first taken away — you may put money in the pockets of one set of Englishmen, but it will be money taken from the pockets of another set of Englishmen, and the greater part will be spilled on the way. Every vote given for Protection is a vote to give Governments the right of robbing Peter to pay Paul and charging the public a handsome commission on the job." – Winston Churchill, *Why I am a Free Trader*, Chapter I in T.W. Stead's journal *Coming Men on Coming Questions* (April 13th, 1905)

My journey to understanding taxation as theft began in 2015 when I learned about the Trivium. The phrase "Taxation is theft" first shocked me in early 2016, as I had never considered taxation in that light. With further research, I came to accept this truth. The Trivium and my commitment to critical thinking were crucial in this realization, primarily since I had been taught from a young age that taxation was a necessary evil. This journey led me to write my first published article in 2016, a seven-page response to an online argument. Everything I've learned and researched since then has only reinforced this understanding.

Taxation, justified as a vital means to fund public services and maintain social order, is the cornerstone of modern governance. However, any attempt to discuss its ethical and moral implications is typically met with fallacious questions like, **who will build the roads?** A closer examination reveals a system that extracts wealth through coercion, disregarding fairness and individual consent. A '**tax**' is a "compulsory contribution" to government revenues. '**Compulsory**' implies "force," and **'contribution'** denotes "a payment." Thus, taxation is not just a payment but a forced one for services we may or may not receive or use. Taxation imposes itself on individuals regardless of their consent. The term 'theft' stems from '**thief**,' which is "one who takes property from another; a robber."

Tax originated from Latin *taxare* as a voluntary fee for specific services, "evaluate, estimate, assess, handle," but evolved into a mandatory, coercive system heavily influenced by practices like the Catholic Church's forced tithing. The Church institutionalized the concept of obligatory contributions, compelling followers to pay tithes -10% of their income- under the threat of spiritual or social consequences. This model of enforced compliance laid the groundwork for modern taxation systems, embedding the principle of violence and force. When the coercive and non-consensual nature of forced tithing and modern taxation is considered, the parallels with theft become undeniable, carrying a weight that challenges the ethical and moral justification of such practices.

TLDR

Tax is a compulsory contribution to government revenues. Compulsory means force, and contribution is a payment. So, taxes are forced payments for services we may or may not use. Theft is taking another person's property without their permission or consent to deprive the rightful owner of it. **Taxation is theft**.

In the Supreme Court case ***McCulloch v. Maryland,* 17 U.S. (4 Wheat.) 316 (1819),** Chief Justice John Marshall stated, "*The power to tax involves the power to destroy*," describing that excessive taxation can lead to Tyranny. The government's ability to tax systematically eliminates competition, consolidates power, and exerts control over nearly every aspect of society. Taxation stifles innovation and personal freedom and drives society toward an inevitable tyrannical breaking point. When the burden of taxation becomes unbearable and the imbalance of power irreparable, the people are often pushed to the edge, sparking revolutions that refresh the endless cycle of statism.

Taxation is fundamentally different from voluntary transactions in a free market. Its reliance on coercion and violence makes it theft. When individuals are forced to give up their earnings under the threat of penalties or imprisonment, taxation's ethical and moral violations become clear. One of the most egregious aspects of taxation is its violation of property rights. In a voluntary transaction, both parties agree to an exchange, ensuring a fair trade of goods, services, or money. Conversely, taxation is imposed unilaterally, regardless of an individual's willingness to participate. Property rights assert that individuals have an inherent right to their labor and earnings, a right that taxation violates. When the government demands a portion of those earnings without consent, it tramples on this natural right, creating injustice.

Additionally, governments rely on their monopoly on violence to enforce tax collection by using police, courts, and other legal systems to ensure compliance through fines, asset seizures, or imprisonment threats. This coercive approach showcases the non-voluntary nature of taxation. Legal backing does not diminish the force involved; it merely institutionalizes it, providing a veneer of legitimacy to actions that would otherwise be condemned if carried out by private individuals.

For example, the Internal Revenue Service (IRS) represents the U.S. federal government's tax enforcement division that directly influences citizens' lives. The Inflation Reduction Act (IRA) of 2022 allocated approximately $80 billion to the IRS, enabling hiring up to 87,000 new employees by 2032. This expansion includes auditors and armed agents equipped with weapons and tactical units. Concurrently, the American Rescue Plan Act of 2021 mandated that third-party payment platforms report transactions exceeding $600, significantly lowering the previous threshold of $20,000 and 200 transactions. These measures predominantly affect citizens and small businesses. In contrast, the elite and large corporations possess the resources to navigate complex tax laws, effectively rendering them "too big to audit." This disparity raises concerns about the equitable application of tax laws and the potential overreach of governmental authority. **Why does the IRS need to hire 87,000 new employees? Are they planning and gearing up for something?**

When we compare taxation to private theft, the parallels become evident. If a private entity were to demand money under threat of violence, it would be labeled as extortion or robbery, which are forms of theft. Now, imagine a scenario where a stranger demands a portion of our earnings under the threat of physical harm. This is what taxation does, albeit through the legal system. The distinction lies in perception, a perception that is shaped by propaganda and fallacious education. Yet, from a moral perspective, the act remains the same: taking one's property without voluntary agreement, a hallmark of theft.

To fully grasp the scope of how governments extract wealth through "legal" means, it is essential to examine the myriad of taxes imposed at federal and state levels. Each tax, whether income, sales, property, or excise, represents a forced payment that citizens are compelled to make under threat of penalties or imprisonment. This system effectively seizes a portion of an individual's earnings, labor, and assets without direct informed consent, aligning taxation with theft than with a fair exchange service fee. By dissecting the different types of taxes levied across the U.S., we can reveal the manipulative tools used to diminish individual property and rights while increasing government control. The government will tax all ways to generate wealth. Remember, the government hates competition. Below is an extensive breakdown of federal and state taxes -does not include local- in place to steal our wealth:

Federal Taxes
- Income Tax – 10% to 37%
- Payroll Tax – 15.3%

- Corporate Income Tax – 21%
- Capital Gains Tax – 0%, 15%, or 20%
- Estate Tax – 18% to 40%
- Gift Tax - 18% to 40%
- Excise Tax – Rates vary
- Federal Insurance Contributions Act (FICA) Tax – 6.2% (Social Security) and 1.45% (Medicare)
- Self-Employment Tax – 15.3%
- Alternative Minimum Tax (AMT) – 26% or 28%
- Unemployment Insurance Tax – 6.0%
- Customs Duties (Tariffs) – 0% to 25%
- Federal Communications Tax – 3%
- Alcohol Tax – Rates vary
- Tobacco Tax – $1.01 per pack
- Gasoline and Diesel Tax – 18.4 cents per gallon
- Air Transportation Tax – 7.5% of the ticket price
- Environmental Taxes – Rates vary
- Foreign Earned Income Tax – 10% to 37%
- Bank Insurance Fund Tax – Rates vary
- Harbor Maintenance Tax – 0.125%
- Oil Spill Liability Tax – $0.09 per barrel
- Federal Land Use Fees – Rates vary

State Taxes
- State Income Tax – 0% to 13.3%
- State Sales Tax – 0% to 7.25%
- Property Tax – 0% to 2.49%
- Corporate Income Tax – 0% to 11.5%
- Estate/Inheritance Tax – 0% to 20%
- Excise Tax – 0% to 20%
- Motor Vehicle Registration Tax – $8 to $800

Taxation is Theft

- Gasoline Tax – 8.95 to 74.1 cents per gallon
- Cigarette Tax – $0.17 to $4.50 per pack
- Alcohol Tax – $0.02 to $35.22 per gallon
- Hotel/Lodging Tax – 0% to 15%
- Rental Car Tax – 2% to 19%
- Telecommunications Tax – 5% to 15%
- Utility Tax – 2% to 10%
- Real Estate Transfer Tax – 0% to 4%
- Severance Tax – Rates vary
- Insurance Premium Tax – 0.5% to 4%
- Amusement and Entertainment Tax – 0% to 10%
- Occupational Privilege Tax – $10 to $52 annually
- Unemployment Insurance Tax – 0% to 6.2%
- Use Tax – 0% to 7.25%
- Fishing and Hunting License Tax – $0 to $80 annually
- Marriage and Civil Union License Tax – $10 to $115
- Divorce Filing Tax – $0 to $400
- Toll Taxes – $1 to $25
- Documentary Stamp Tax – 0.35% to 2%
- Admissions Tax – 0% to 10%
- Pollution Control Tax – Rates vary
- Transportation Improvement Tax – 0.25% to 1%
- Educational Fund Tax – 0.25% to 2%
- Local Option Tax – 0% to 3%
- Business Franchise Tax – 0% to 9.99%
- Gross Receipts Tax – 0% to 5%
- Payroll Tax – 0.1% to 1.5%
- Special District Tax – 0.25% to 2%
- Emergency Communication Tax (911 Fee) – $0.50 to $3 per month
- Prepared Food Tax – 4% to 11%

- Timber Yield Tax – 2% to 5%
- Hospital Tax – 0.5% to 2%
- Petroleum Business Tax – 0.05% to 8%
- Renewable Energy Tax – 0.25% to 2%
- Stormwater Utility Fee – $3 to $15 per month
- Cannabis Tax – 10% to 37%
- Personal Property Tax – 0.1% to 3.5%
- Motor Fuel Tax – 5 cents to 38 cents per gallon
- Jet Fuel Tax – 0.1 cents to 10 cents per gallon
- Tire Recycling Tax – $0.50 to $5 per tire
- Beverage Container Deposit Tax – 5 cents to 10 cents per container
- Hazardous Waste Tax – $50 to $200 per ton
- Landfill Tax – $2 to $50 per ton
- Gaming Tax – 6% to 35%
- Public Utility Commission Tax – 0.5% to 4%
- Bank Franchise Tax – 0.25% to 12%
- Sugar-Sweetened Beverage Tax – $0.01 to $0.02 per ounce
- Capital Stock Tax – 0.1% to 1%
- Recording Fees Tax – $0.50 to $50 per document
- Firearm Transfer Tax – $10 to $200
- Aircraft Registration Tax – $25 to $300 annually
- Boat and Watercraft Tax – 0.5% to 10%

Historical Perspective

Understanding the historical context of taxation is crucial. Taxation has historically favored the ruling elites at the expense of the general population. During the feudal era, taxation was mandatory tributes from serfs to landowners and the state. Serfs, bound to the land they worked, were required to surrender a substantial portion of their produce or labor to the ruling class. This system entrenched economic inequality, ensuring that the working class remained in perpetual poverty while the "elites" amassed wealth.

In colonial times, European powers imposed heavy taxes on colonized nations, using wealth extraction to fund their imperial ambitions. This was a key issue during the American Revolution. A notable example is Britain's salt tax in India, which forced Indians to pay exorbitant fees for necessities. The salt tax exacerbated poverty and symbolized colonial oppression, yet it also sparked resistance movements such as Mahatma Gandhi's iconic Salt March in 1930. This act of disobedience, a testament to the resilience of the oppressed, illustrates the exploitative nature of colonial taxation and its devastating impact on local populations.

In the modern era, taxation disproportionately affects the working and middle classes, while the wealthy utilize tax loopholes and offshore accounts to shield their wealth. Revelations such as the Panama and Paradise Papers have exposed how global elites evade taxes, shifting the financial burden onto ordinary citizens. This dynamic perpetuates economic inequality, as those with fewer resources are forced to bear the brunt of funding public services while the wealthy exploit systemic advantages.

For example, Warren Buffett donated $750 million in 2022 to his family's charitable foundations. Additionally, in June 2024, Buffett donated over $4 billion to the Bill & Melinda Gates Foundation and $1.3 billion to four family-led charities. By donating to non-profit charities and organizations, Buffett can write the donations as tax write-offs, lowering his tax burden on taxable income while avoiding Estate taxes for his family as they can use the funds through their charities. On top of the tax benefits, Buffett's public relations image makes him seem like a philanthropist billionaire because he donates billions to charities, even if the charities are only a front for laundering money to avoid taxes. To add to the complexity of taxing the super-rich and wealthy, Buffett's financial assets are so massive and significant it would take considerable resources -auditors, investigators, lawyers, etc.- to conduct full audits with taxpayer funds. There is no return on investment when auditing individuals like Buffet or President Trump. These examples stress the urgent need for systemic change as taxation continues to prioritize the interests of elites over the well-being of the broader population. **If an individual is too big to audit, why is anyone audited? Do you believe the 87,000 new IRS employees are being hired to audit the elite?**

Economic Impact

Taxation has profound economic consequences that devalue individual labor and savings. For example, direct taxation on income reduces the amount of money individuals take home, while indirect taxes on goods and services increase the cost of living. These factors can undermine individual financial growth and exacerbate economic disparities, creating barriers to individual prosperity and broader economic advancement.

Governments reduce the incentive to work harder or take entrepreneurial risks by taxing earnings, mainly when high marginal tax rates are imposed. These high rates can weigh heavily on individual decisions, discouraging workers and business owners from seeking promotions or expanding their businesses due to the diminishing returns on additional income. This disincentive impacts individuals and hampers overall economic productivity and growth, leading to the "need" for concepts like Universal Basic Income (UBI). However, this aligns more with the Broken Window Fallacy, where the government causes the problem and then offers a solution that only worsens things, making people more reliant on the government.

Even though exorbitant taxation and government overreach drive these issues, governments and proponents often propose UBI to solve economic inequality, automation-driven job losses, and financial instability. The argument is that UBI could eliminate poverty and create economic stability by providing citizens with a fixed monthly income. However, UBI increases the cost of living, reduces the dollar's value, and acts as a tool of control, fostering dependence on government handouts. If the government can give it to us, it can take it away, forcing reliance on the government. This reliance ensures continued public support and consolidation of power, leaving most citizens dependent and obedient. The COVID19 pandemic started to get citizens hooked on the appeal of cash assistance programs, such as the CARES Act of 2020 stimulus checks. Still, it also demonstrated how such measures can devalue currency and expand government control. A UBI system may appear benevolent but risks creating a populace increasingly tethered to centralized governance, compromising individual autonomy and economic freedom, and significantly increasing the national debt to cover it. This concern cannot be overlooked or taken lightly.

Inflation, usually disregarded, acts as a hidden form of taxation that further devalues individual wealth. When governments print money to cover deficits, it leads to inflation, weakening the currency's purchasing power and savings -supply versus demand. Citizens are hit twice: once through direct taxation and again as inflation drives up the cost of goods and services. For example, persistent inflation in recent years has made necessities increasingly unaffordable for many households, diminishing the value of their savings and forcing them to bear the financial consequences of the government's fiscal mismanagement, which is lessened for the elites due to the wealth they have already amassed. This economic burden drives society toward accepting things like UBI systems and relying on the government for support. The urgency of this issue is stressed by the fact that due to the government printing more money for the COVID19 pandemic stimulus package in 2020, inflation rapidly increased, and the dollar's value was devalued by 18.27% within five years. The percentage of value lost = **([Final Value – Initial Value] / Final Value) x 100.**

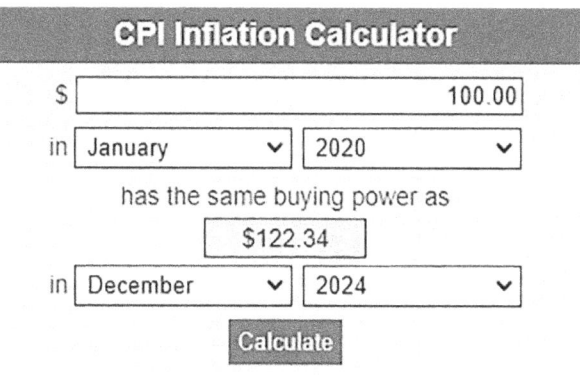

Source: https://www.bls.gov/data/inflation_calculator.htm

Adding to the complexity of taxation and inflation, the government must pay interest on the newly printed money, classified as public debt, to the Federal Reserve, a consortium of private banks in partnership with the government. This, in turn, adds to the taxpayer's load, as they are responsible for the interest payments on public debt, further transferring wealth. Governments resorting to borrowing for their expenses accumulate substantial debts that must be repaid using taxpayer money. The U.S. currently allocates over a trillion dollars annually -roughly 3%- for interest payments on its 35 trillion in national debt. These payments have more than doubled in the last decade. The Congressional Budget Office (CBO) reported that by 2034, over 75% of the federal deficit's increase will be caused by these interest payments. This currently equates to roughly $2.8 billion a day in interest payments. This sets in motion a cycle where future generations grapple with the long-term financial repercussions of the current government's wasteful and endless spending.

Regressive taxes, such as sales and value-added taxes (VAT), unfairly burden lower-income individuals who allocate a significant portion of their income to essential goods and services. These taxes worsen wealth inequality by placing a heavier financial and economic burden on those who can least afford it. For example, a flat sales tax on groceries or utilities significantly impacts a low-income household. In contrast, high-income households are relatively unaffected, deepening economic disparities and limiting upward mobility.

Government Overreach

Taxation is framed as a necessary evil to support social infrastructure and public services, but in reality, it is an unjust system that enables government overreach. A prime example is the understanding that the government has no duty to protect or serve individuals, so there is no duty to maintain and support social infrastructure and public services through taxation. Taxation allows authorities to violate individual freedoms and natural rights under the pretense of serving the public interest. From property rights to large-scale redistributions of wealth, taxation has been weaponized to finance activities that many citizens neither support nor benefit from, sparking a sense of ethical and moral outrage at this injustice.

Property taxes and eminent domain are examples of unjustly undermining private ownership. Property taxes ensure that individuals never genuinely own their land; failure to pay these taxes results in the government's seizure of the property, effectively turning ownership into a form of leasing and renting from the government. Eminent domain compounds this injustice by granting governments the authority to confiscate private property for public use, usually compensating owners below market or "fair" value. Such practices flagrantly violate the foundational principles of property rights, turning what should be protected personal assets into resources perpetually vulnerable to the government's control.

Taxation also leads to a profound misuse of taxpayer funds. For example, the Iraq War, which cost U.S. taxpayers over $2 trillion, was launched under contentious and, later, widely disputed justifications. These expenditures diverted resources from pressing domestic needs such as healthcare, education, and infrastructure, further alienating taxpayers forced to fund interventions they may have opposed. This misallocation of resources is not just a theoretical concern but a pressing issue that affects us all, creating a sense of betrayal among taxpayers.

Another troubling example of taxation enabling government overreach is the redistribution of wealth through crony capitalism - government-run capitalism. During the 2008 financial crisis, over $2.2 trillion in taxpayer dollars were funneled into corporate subsidies and bailouts for large financial institutions. The actual total, with additional commitments and guarantees, made the overall taxpayer cost $16.8 trillion. While these measures were justified as necessary to stabilize the economy, corporations were deemed "too big to fail," which left individual citizens to bear the economic fallout. Homeowners lost their properties, small businesses shuttered, and unemployment skyrocketed, while the financial institutions responsible for the crisis were shielded from accountability using public funds. This is only a small but grim example of the injustice and corruption in the system.

Taxation becomes particularly argumentative when vast sums of taxpayer funds are allocated as foreign aid to countries like Ukraine and Israel while urgent domestic crises are neglected. Billions of taxpayer dollars are annually sent abroad under the pretext of geopolitical strategy or international stability, yet communities within the U.S. face ongoing struggles with crumbling infrastructure, inadequate disaster relief, and systemic issues like homelessness.

For example, residents devastated by Hurricane Katrina, the Flint, Michigan water crisis, and Hurricane Helene endure prolonged hardship with insufficient federal and state action and support. This contrast shows a misalignment in priorities, as taxpayer money is diverted to foreign interests while domestic issues persist unaddressed. Such practices deepen public frustration and lend credence to the argument that taxation does not function as a tool for the public good but as an instrument of exploitation and economic marginalization.

These examples remind us that taxation extends beyond its intended purpose of serving the public good. Instead, it is a tool that facilitates government actions, infringing upon individual rights, misallocating resources, and prioritizing corporate or political interests over the needs and desires of individual citizens. This dynamic raises questions about taxation's ethical and moral limits and the government's role in managing public funds.

The sheer scope and scale of federal taxation are staggering. By 2015, federal tax laws and regulations had swelled to over 10 million words, creating a labyrinth that burdens citizens and businesses with compliance costs and confusion, making it near impossible for the average citizen to understand what is happening to them. This complexity not only obscures the true nature of taxation but also disproportionately affects those without the resources to navigate its intricacies, solidifying inequality in the name of a public need and the greater good.

The U.S. government's financial mismanagement illustrates the deep flaws within its operations. As of December 2024, the national debt surpassed $35 trillion, placing an enormous burden on taxpayers forced to shoulder the costs of servicing this escalating liability. This debt is forced upon all citizens with no say in how it is spent, equal to over $100,000 for every man, woman, and child with a social security number or over $270,000 per taxpayer. **At what point will this crushing debt cause a complete economic collapse? Or is that the plan -"trust the plan"- to further the progression toward Tyranny by increasing the reliance on the government?**

The DoD has faced a long history of financial mismanagement, with its first failed audit revealed by Defense Secretary Donald Rumsfeld on national news on September 10th, 2001 -just one day before the tragic events of 9/11. This audit uncovered $2.4 trillion in unaccounted expenditures, a disclosure eclipsed by the following national crisis. However, the issue of financial mismanagement did not end there. In 2016, the DoD reported $6.5 trillion in wrongful adjustments to its financial statements, reflecting deeply rooted systemic failures. However, mainstream media focused on the presidential battle between President Trump and Hilary Clinton, completely ignoring the unaccounted-for trillions. This illustrates the mainstream media's role in shaping public perception of government actions. Between 1996 and 2015, an additional $2.2 trillion in unaccounted-for transactions were identified. By 2022, audits exposed another $2.4 trillion in unauditable transactions, accentuating the persistent lack of fiscal accountability within one of the government's largest and most critical institutions. The 2023 audit further revealed another $2.7 trillion in unauditable transactions, with $1.4 trillion classified as "unsupported." These figures bring the cumulative total of unaccounted funds within the DoD to a rough estimation of $10 trillion to $12 trillion when accounting for overlap in findings.

These figures are a disturbing trend of financial opacity and mismanagement, raising profound questions about oversight and the ethical stewardship of taxpayer dollars. With trillions of dollars effectively disappearing into bureaucratic voids, the lack of accountability within the DoD emphasizes systemic vulnerabilities. This unchecked progression of financial mismanagement directly impacts the average citizen, who, conversely, is forced to pay and account for everything or face an authoritarian government that has a monopoly on violence and force.

At the state level, California's fiscal mismanagement regarding a $20 billion federal loan for unemployment costs during the COVID19 pandemic has created significant financial strain for businesses and taxpayers, with long-term implications. The state borrowed the funds after mandating widespread business closures, leaving many jobless, but failed to repay the loan on time despite receiving $27 billion in federal stimulus money and boasting a nearly $100 billion budget surplus during that period. Instead of using the funds to address the debt, state leaders allocated them elsewhere, leading to massive budget deficits in 2023 and 2024. Consequently, California now requires businesses to cover the shortfall through increased payroll taxes, starting with an extra $21 per employee and rising incrementally each year -$42 in 2026, $63 in 2027, etc.- until the debt is cleared. Compounding the issue is that over $32 billion of unemployment benefits distributed during the pandemic were fraudulent, and the state pays $1 billion annually in interest on the debt. This failure of fiscal governance emphasizes the long-term burden on businesses and taxpayers caused by state governments' poor financial decisions and how the government looks only to solve issues it creates by taxing its citizens further. **If taking 100% of the labor and earnings of an individual is slavery, at what percentage is it not slavery?**

This constant lack of oversight and accountability raises ethical, moral, and practical concerns at the federal and state levels. **How can the government justify extracting more revenue and wealth from its citizens when trillions of taxpayer dollars are mishandled or vanish without explanation or accountability?** The contrast between the government's demands for tax compliance and its inability to manage its finances responsibly emphasizes the fallacious belief that it can efficiently and transparently manage public funds for the greater good.

Taxation in Practice

The Whiskey Rebellion, a significant event in early U.S. history, is an example of taxation's true nature. In 1791, the federal government imposed an excise tax on distilled spirits, a move that disproportionately affected small farmers in Pennsylvania who relied on whiskey production for their livelihoods. The tax was seen as an unjust burden on rural communities struggling economically, sparking widespread protests and resistance. When peaceful efforts to repeal the tax failed, the rebellion escalated, culminating in the deployment of 13,000 federal troops under President George Washington to suppress the protesters. This use of military force to enforce tax compliance revealed the extent to which governments are willing to prioritize revenue collection over addressing the grievances of their citizens, setting a precedent for the enforcement of taxation through coercion and violence. This hypocritical act came only a few decades after the U.S. won its independence from Tyranny, which was sparked by a tyrannical government overtaxing its citizens.

Eric Garner's death in 2014 brought attention to the overlooked human cost of tax enforcement. Police confronted Garner for allegedly selling untaxed cigarettes, a minor infraction rooted in the government's effort to maintain control over revenue streams. During the encounter, Garner was placed in a chokehold -a maneuver prohibited by police policy- which led to his death. This tragic event shows how taxation, even at its most minor scales, can lead to criminalization and deadly outcomes. Garner's case is part of a broader issue of how governments use aggressive enforcement actions to demand compliance, even when the infraction poses no significant threat to public safety.

In 2016, the U.S. Marshals arrested Paul Aker for failing to repay a 30-year-old student loan of $1,500 -borrowed in 1987- revealing another facet of taxation's tyrannical overreach. Law enforcement pursued Aker using full combat gear and "weapons of war" to repay the loan he had defaulted on. His arrest warrant was issued for failure to appear in federal court. After his arrest, he was forced to sign a repayment plan for the original $1,500 in debt. This incident illustrates how government enforcement extends beyond taxes to other financial obligations, prioritizing debt collection over the well-being of individuals. The use of armed officers to address a civil matter is an extreme measure that governments employ to secure revenue, raising questions about the ethics and morality of using public resources to target individuals struggling with financial burdens. **What do you think the total cost was for the government to deploy the officers and support personnel to find and force Aker to sign a piece of paper?**

Together, these examples illustrate tax enforcement's pervasive and oppressive nature. From military interventions in the Whiskey

Rebellion to the tragic consequences of policing minor infractions like Eric Garner's case and the deployment of law enforcement for student debt collection, these incidents reveal the lengths governments will go to maintain control over revenue. Such practices challenge the rhetoric of taxation as a benign or neutral system, instead exposing it as a tyrannical tool and function of an oppressive government.

In its current form, taxation operates as a system of legalized theft that violates individual rights, perpetuates inequality, and drives governments toward Tyranny. By coercing individuals to surrender their wealth, governments prioritize their interests and agendas over the well-being of the citizens. Taxation provides the financial means for unchecked government expansion, enabling policies that eat away at individual rights, such as mass surveillance, militarized policing, and the funding of proxy wars. Taxation diminishes the value of personal labor and savings. Combined with inflation and public debt, it facilitates the continued transfer of wealth from individuals to centralized authorities and their corporate beneficiaries. This concentration of power encourages crony capitalism, where taxpayer money is funneled to private interests, creating a system that benefits elites. In a tax-free society, individuals would retain control over the fruits of their labor and the direction of their lives, fostering a sense of empowerment and optimism. As long as the government continues to use taxation as a tool of control, there will be a steady progression toward Tyranny.

"When a government taxes you, it takes something you own without your consent. That's exactly what a thief does. The main difference is that the thief is breaking the law, whereas the government is (usually) taking your money legally." – David R. Henderson, *The Joy of Freedom: An Economist's Odyssey, Financial Times/Prentice Hall* (2002)

Engineered Consent

"*Autonomy has never been recognized as a legally protectable interest. It has been vindicated only as byproduct of protection of two other interests – bodily security as protected by rules against consented contact, and bodily well-being as protected by rules governing professional competence.*" – Marjorie Shultz, *Informed Consent: Legal Theory and Clinical Practice* (2001)

Consent is a fundamental principle essential to any voluntary interaction. It hinges on transparency, free will, and the absence of coercion, ensuring that individuals are respected and in control of their choices. '**Consent**' is the *voluntary acceptance and agreement in sentiment in a given situation*. It is rooted in individual autonomy, mutual agreement, and voluntary acceptance. It requires truthful communication and a lack of coercion and manipulation, distinct from persuasion. Understanding the difference between manipulation and persuasion is not just essential; it's empowering. It equips individuals with the knowledge to make decisions without external influence, strengthening their autonomy and control.

Questions
- What distinguishes consensual sex from rape? **Consent**
- What differentiates taking someone's money or property from theft? **Consent**

Informed Consent

Informed consent is particularly critical in contexts such as medical decision-making and research. It ensures that individuals receive comprehensive and accurate information about the risks, benefits, and alternatives associated with a given choice, thereby promoting transparency. This principle respects individuals' Right to Autonomy by empowering them to make decisions based on a clear understanding of the implications. For example, patients agreeing to a surgical procedure must be fully briefed on the potential outcomes, risks, and recovery process. Any failure to disclose pertinent information weakens the integrity of the consent and exposes individuals to unintended harm, rendering the agreement invalid. When informed consent is made invalid, it can lead to exploitative practices, where individuals are misled or pressured into choices they do not fully understand, which can lead to the death of the individual. When individuals are purposely misled or pressured, it becomes "engineered consent," which raises significant ethical and moral concerns because it subverts the principles that make consent valid.

Engineered Consent

Engineered consent is a term used to describe the manipulation or coercion of an individual's actions to obtain a desired outcome. Engineered consent manipulates individuals or groups into agreeing to something they might otherwise reject if fully informed. This is done by exploiting psychological techniques, providing misinformation, or targeting emotional appeals -logical fallacies. By prioritizing manipulation over truth, engineered consent shifts power away from individuals and into the hands of those controlling the rhetoric, creating an imbalance that can have far-reaching consequences for the individual and society.

Engineered consent, a concept introduced by Edward Bernays, reveals how individuals can be subtly manipulated into agreement through propaganda, psychological tactics, or the deliberate withholding of essential information. Governments expand on these methods by employing various intimidation, threats, violence, and coercion strategies while interpreting silence as implicit consent. Unlike informed consent, engineered consent seeks to manipulate and control behavior to serve the interests of those in power, leading to harmful outcomes.

For example, government-funded advertising campaigns -like the NFL's display of patriotism- exploit emotional appeals or present biased information, leading consumers to make choices that align more with corporate and government goals than their interests. In politics, engineered consent involves the selective presentation of limited facts or sophist rhetoric to influence public opinion without providing the full scope of information necessary for informed consent.

The attack on informed consent and the rise of engineered consent represents a troubling progression from individual autonomy to tyrannical, manipulated agreements. This shift stresses the importance of protecting truth, transparency, and voluntary acceptance. It's not just a matter of ethics or moral credibility; it's a matter of preserving the integrity of consent in all areas of life. The urgency of this task cannot be overstated, as it is crucial for maintaining individual autonomy and preventing the spread of engineered consent.

Obtaining Consent

Propaganda is a powerful tool that leverages selective misinformation, disinformation, and emotional appeals that shape prevailing societal rhetoric. During World War I, governments employed propaganda to rally public support for the war effort, using posters and media to portray enemies as subhuman threats, thereby justifying military actions. In more recent times, mainstream media rhetoric during the COVID19 pandemic exemplified information control. Government and corporate interests aligned to selectively present data about vaccines and lockdowns, omitting and censoring opposing viewpoints or alternative healthcare strategies. This approach framed the public rhetoric in a way that aligned with predetermined objectives, subtly guiding collective opinion without full transparency. In the digital age, social media platforms and targeted advertising have become powerful tools for engineered consent, as they can selectively present information and manipulate emotions to guide user behavior.

Sophistry manipulates facts and terms to create deceptive arguments, relying on logical fallacies to engineer consent. Tactics such as presenting false dichotomies or appealing to authority limit critical examination and enforce acceptance of approved rhetoric. A historical example is the Gulf of Tonkin Incident in 1964, where U.S. forces claimed two unprovoked attacks by North Vietnam to justify escalating the Vietnam War. Subsequent investigations revealed that the second incident was fabricated, demonstrating how false rhetoric can manipulate public perception and support for controversial actions. Such examples also show how engineered consent can rely on lies and misinformation to achieve political goals.

Governments exploit fear, a potent motivator in manufacturing consent, to push through policies that would otherwise face resistance. After the 9/11 attacks, the Patriot Act of 2001 was passed with broad public and political support, leveraging the fear of terrorism to justify mass surveillance and the limiting of individual rights. Coercion similarly inhibits genuine consent by pressuring individuals into compliance.

For example, during the COVID19 pandemic, employer mandates for vaccinations -medical procedures- left employees with the choice of either complying or losing their jobs, creating a scenario where agreement was achieved under duress rather than voluntary informed consent. Many state governments used emergency powers to impose regulations on business owners, compelling them to enforce mask mandates or vaccination requirements or risk being shut down and losing their business licenses. This approach obscured the source of these mandates and restrictions, complicating obtaining valid informed consent while making it look like private businesses were making private decisions. This should make us all more aware of potential future manipulation during times of crisis.

Monetary or social incentives can further distort informed consent by introducing external pressures that override individual autonomy. For example, lotteries, financial incentives, or offering free food and services during the COVID19 pandemic for obedience to accepting a vaccine capitalized on economic hardships and social expectations to drive participation. These methods exploited vulnerabilities and social dynamics to achieve desired outcomes, blurring the line between informed and engineered consent. Peer pressure further reinforced this dynamic, as individuals faced social stigmatization for non-obedience, effectively coercing them into decisions that may not have occurred with informed consent. By controlling information, leveraging fear, and exploiting social dynamics, governments guide collective behavior to serve their objectives while maintaining the illusion of public consent.

Case Law

Engineered consent has been examined in various legal contexts. Several landmark cases demonstrate the importance of ensuring consent is informed, voluntary, and free from manipulation or coercion:

Miranda v. Arizona, **384 U.S. 436 (1966)** is a case involving a suspect's right to remain silent and have an attorney present during police interrogations, becoming pivotal in addressing engineered consent within law enforcement. The case established the precedent for police to inform individuals of their rights during police interrogations. By mandating the disclosure of these rights, the ruling sought to prevent coerced confessions obtained through intimidation or manipulation. This decision was critical in reducing the power imbalance during police interrogations and sought to ensure individuals' voluntary agreement or confession.

Cruzan v. Director, Missouri Department of Health, **497 U.S. 261 (1990)** is a case that highlights the importance of informed consent in medical decisions. The case involved a patient's right to refuse life-sustaining treatment, with the Supreme Court ruling that such decisions must be based on clear evidence of the individual's wishes. This case stressed that consent in healthcare must be informed and free from coercion, placing an ethical obligation on medical professionals to provide patients with comprehensive information about risks, benefits, and alternatives. It reinforced the idea that patients must retain autonomy over their medical choices.

Doe v. Chao, **540 U.S. 614 (2004)** is a case that addressed privacy violations and the unauthorized use of Social Security numbers, finding explicit and informed consent necessary before handling personal information. The plaintiff argued that their data had been mishandled without proper consent, leading to harm. This case challenged practices where consent was implied or obtained through misleading tactics, stressing the importance of transparency and accountability when dealing with sensitive personal data. It sets a precedent for protecting privacy rights and ensuring that individuals are fully informed about how their information is used.

Together, these cases illustrate the supposed judicial system's role in upholding the principles of informed and voluntary consent. These law enforcement, healthcare, and data privacy rulings demonstrate the efforts to address coercive or deceptive practices. Despite these legal precedents, governments violate informed consent through policies and practices, creating systemic overreach and diminishing the valuable impact of informed consent.

Applications and Implications

One of the most glaring examples of engineered consent is political manipulation. Governments frequently use selective and sophist rhetoric to justify controversial policies, bypassing public scrutiny. An example is the "weapons of mass destruction" rhetoric employed to garner support for the 2003 invasion of Iraq. Despite later evidence disproving the claim, it successfully rallied public and political backing for military action.

Even government-approved education is a tool for engineering consent, as curricula frequently present historical or scientific rhetoric aligned with government goals and interests. This approach subtly shapes students' perspectives, leaving little room for critical thought or dissent, and normalizes prevailing ideologies, leaving individuals uninformed and unable to give informed consent.

The implications of engineered consent are far-reaching. The 1972 Watergate scandal revealed widespread government deception and demonstrated how engineered consent led to public disillusionment. Ethical violations further illustrate the dangers of engineered consent. Historical cases like the Tuskegee Syphilis Study (1932–1972) show how withholding critical information and manipulating individuals violate human rights and ethical principles. Moreover, the widespread use of engineered consent normalizes coercion, making it increasingly difficult for individuals to discern rights violations. As coercive tactics become commonplace, resistance to these practices weakens, perpetuating cycles of manipulation and control. Addressing these issues requires a concerted effort to promote transparency, encourage critical thinking, and hold those responsible for manipulation accountable.

Engineered consent is a destructive force that subverts the principles of autonomy and informed decision-making. It is used as a tool for governments and corporations to amass power and limit individual rights. These entities disrupt ethical governance by manipulating information, exploiting vulnerabilities, and prioritizing control over the truth. This sets the stage for systemic coercion. This manipulation breeds compliance and conditions populations to accept authority without question, paving the way for the unchecked expansion of governmental power. Engineered consent justifies policies that curtail freedoms and rights, centralize control, and suppress opposition under the appearance of the collective good, hastening the march toward Tyranny.

"The conscious and intelligent manipulation of the organized habits and opinions of the masses is an important element in democratic society. Those who manipulate this unseen mechanism of society constitute an invisible government which is the true ruling power of our country. We are governed, our minds are molded, our tastes formed, our ideas suggested, largely by men we have never heard of. This is a logical result of the way in which our democratic society is organized. Vast numbers of human beings must cooperate in this manner if they are to live together as a smoothly functioning society." – Edward Bernays, *Propaganda* (1928)

Psychological Operations

"If you give a man the correct information for seven years, he may believe the incorrect information on the first day of the eighth year when it is necessary, from your point of view, that he should do so. Your first job is to build the credibility and the authenticity of your propaganda, and persuade the enemy to trust you although you are his enemy." – A *Psychological Warfare Casebook, Operations Research Office, Johns Hopkins University Baltimore* (1958)

Psychological operations (PSYOPs) and manipulation are not just tools for the government but strategic instruments meticulously designed to shape behavior, influence opinions, and control individuals, groups, and societal decisions. These operations are not haphazard but carefully planned and executed. Propaganda, deception, engineered consent, terrorism, and psychological tactics are employed to achieve specific objectives. PSYOPs rely on carefully crafted messaging and psychological techniques to exploit vulnerabilities, reinforce rhetoric, and suppress opposition, focusing on manipulation over persuasion.

The U.S. government actively collaborates with private entities to expand its PSYOP capabilities. Contracts like the Joint Enterprise Defense Infrastructure (JEDI) and Commercial Cloud Enterprise (C2E) involve tech giants such as Microsoft, Amazon, and Google, which provide infrastructure for cloud computing and data analysis. These partnerships allow intelligence agencies to analyze massive amounts of information and data, further enhancing their ability to conduct PSYOPs. Integrating advanced technologies like machine learning and artificial intelligence (AI) is not just a trend but a crucial development that enables these agencies to refine their strategies, tailoring misinformation and disinformation campaigns to target audiences with unprecedented precision and success. For example, in 2025, President Trump announced a $500 billion taxpayer investment in a new company called the **Stargate Project**, which aims to revolutionize an AI infrastructure for OpenAI within the U.S., further establishing tools that can be used for tyranny and aligning the U.S. with globalist agendas.

The COVID19 pandemic allowed governments and corporations to deploy PSYOPs globally, leveraging fear and uncertainty to enforce compliance with public health measures. Messaging strategies focus on worst-case scenarios, death tolls, and alarming statistics, amplifying public anxiety. This fear-based communication was used to justify sweeping restrictions, such as lockdowns and mask and vaccine mandates while suppressing alternative perspectives and approaches. Social media platforms and fact-checking organizations played pivotal roles, censoring dissenting opinions and bolstering the government-approved rhetoric, often labeling them as "misinformation" or "disinformation." The lack of transparency and open dialogue caused many to question whether these measures were genuinely based on truthful science or served broader political and corporate agendas. This manipulation of public fear during the pandemic showcases how crises can be exploited to consolidate authority and control disguised as a need for public safety and welfare.

PSYOPs are not isolated efforts but part of a vast, interconnected ecosystem involving governments, private corporations, academic institutions, and intelligence agencies worldwide. By exploiting tools like sockpuppet accounts, deepfakes, and institutional propaganda, these operations aim to dictate global rhetoric, control dissent, and consolidate power. While justified as necessary for national security or public welfare, the actions we see today raise philosophical and ethical concerns. The urgency of the issue is underscored by the increasing frequency of these operations being deployed against foreign and domestic populations. These tools are not unexpected but a clear sign of a global effort to move the world toward Tyranny and a wholly controlled surveillance system to keep all populations and citizens obedient.

PSYOPs are strategic and deliberate activities designed to influence emotions, motives, and objective reasoning in targeted audiences to achieve specific and significant strategic objectives. The U.S. DoD defines PSYOPs as "planned operations to convey selected information and indicators to foreign and domestic audiences to influence their emotions, motives, objective reasoning, and ultimately the behavior of governments, organizations, groups, and individuals." These operations can range from subtle messaging to overt propaganda and counterpropaganda campaigns, using media broadcasts, leaflet drops, or digital outreach to craft and reinforce desired rhetoric and actions. In extreme cases, terrorism is employed to achieve the desired outcome. PSYOPs operate on the principle of exploiting psychological vulnerabilities to induce compliance, agreement, or desired behavioral outcomes without the target's explicit awareness of the influence being exerted upon them.

Manipulation involves intentionally using deceptive or exploitative tactics to control or sway individuals, groups, or societies. While PSYOPs claim legitimacy under national security, public welfare, or the preservation of stability, manipulation tends to disregard ethical and moral considerations, prioritizing attaining power or advantage over adherence to truth or fairness. It leaves individuals unaware of how their perceptions and actions are shaped and never for their benefit. Manipulation is an integral part of PSYOPs. For example, during wartime, PSYOPs may disseminate exaggerated or false claims to demoralize enemy forces or rally domestic support.

Understanding the mechanics and ethical considerations of PSYOPs and manipulation is not just important but essential in an era when information warfare and mass communication technologies have amplified their reach and impact. As societies grapple with the pervasive influence of these tactics, scrutinizing their applications and implications becomes increasingly essential.

Types of PSYOPs

PSYOPs employ various mechanisms and tools designed to influence perceptions and behaviors. These methods leverage emotional, cultural, and cognitive vulnerabilities to shape the actions of individuals and groups. Each type offers a unique pathway to controlling thought and decisions while aligning with strategic or political objectives.

Terrorism

The terms '**terror**' and '**terrorism**' defined as "government intimidation," originated during the *Reign of Terror* (1793–1794) in France, where the government perpetrated systematic violence and intimidation against its citizens to consolidate power and suppress opposition and disobedience. Fear is a key tool and aspect of terrorism used to control populations and enforce compliance. By this definition and context, the U.S. government, with its extensive history of using intimidation, coercion, and violence to achieve political ends for foreign and domestic citizens, could be considered the largest terrorist organization in the world. From its expansive military interventions abroad to its domestic surveillance programs and law enforcement practices, the U.S. government has systematically employed fear and force to maintain authority and suppress opposition internationally. This is not to say that other non-government institutions and individuals could not conduct terroristic acts, only that the U.S. government is the largest perpetrator of it.

This concept and definition of terrorism have evolved in the modern era. According to the FBI, terrorism encompasses activities involving violent or life-threatening acts that violate federal or state law and are intended to intimidate or coerce a civilian population, influence government policies through intimidation or coercion, or affect governmental conduct through mass destruction, assassination, or kidnapping. In 2019, the FBI began categorizing conspiracy theorists as domestic terrorists, equating skepticism of government-approved rhetoric with acts of terror. This shift in definition from the root to the modern era reflects how the term 'terrorism' has been weaponized to stigmatize and silence opposition, distancing it from "government intimidation," further entrenching governmental authority while censoring free thought and open discourse.

Propaganda

Propaganda is a key aspect of PSYOPs, involving the dissemination of biased or misleading information to promote a specific cause or viewpoint. By utilizing emotional appeals, selective facts, and repetition, propaganda aims to embed a desired rhetoric and action within the public consciousness. For example, during Nazi Germany's regime, Joseph Goebbels' Ministry of Propaganda employed films, posters, and speeches to demonize Jewish people and glorify the Aryan race. These messages nurtured widespread public support for genocidal policies, demonstrating the powerful and dangerous potential of propaganda when used to manipulate social beliefs. This is similar to the Disinformation Governance Board (DGB), under the DHS, that President Biden created in 2022. Luckily, this board was quickly disbanded after significant public backlash.

Establishing propaganda-focused entities such as the Corporation for Public Broadcasting (CPB) demonstrates how governments institutionalize PSYOPs in the name of public service. Funded by taxpayers, organizations like the Public Broadcasting Service (PBS) and National Public Radio (NPR) significantly influence public rhetoric, aligning their messaging with governmental objectives. Similarly, repealing the Smith-Mundt Act in 2013 through the National Defense Authorization Act (NDAA) allowed the U.S. government to officially direct propaganda toward domestic citizens, further integrating PSYOPs into everyday mainstream media consumption.

Covertly, between 2007 and 2011, the Pentagon paid the British public relations firm Bell Pottinger over $500 million to create fake Al-Qaeda propaganda videos as part of covert PSYOPs campaigns during the Iraq War. These operations included producing videos designed to resemble authentic terrorist content, some of which reportedly included staged beheading footage. **Do you remember these videos and how the public reacted to them?**

The aim was to manipulate public rhetoric and garner support for the ongoing war effort by amplifying the perceived threat of terrorism from the Middle East and justifying U.S. military actions in the region. This shows the lengths governments go to sway public perception and control rhetoric.

Disinformation and Mainstream Media

Disinformation deliberately spreads false information to mislead, confuse, and deceive targeted individuals. This involves constructing elaborate false rhetoric or staging events -false flags- to reinforce the misinformation. While such tactics have been effectively used in military contexts, their use against unsuspecting domestic populations raises profound ethical, moral, and legal concerns. When governments deploy disinformation against their citizens, they violate fundamental rights. This breach of trust distorts public discourse and collapses the supposedly foundational principles of democracy, further pushing government toward Tyranny.

The rise of "fake news" as a mainstream concept further exacerbates this issue, with media outlets like Fox, CNN, and MSNBC accused of spreading misleading or biased information on an ongoing basis, which leaves citizens vulnerable to manipulation and less equipped to discern truth from propaganda. The term gained widespread attention in 2016 when a list of "fake news" sites compiled by Professor Melissa Zimdars of Merrimack College went viral, sparking intense debates about media credibility and the manipulation of information. Her list included sites like the Free Thought Project, which publishes honest and factual news articles that focus on alternative rhetoric instead of only government-approved rhetoric. Additionally, Professor Zimdars' list included Liberty Movement Radio (LMR), which I co-owned then, and hosted multiple podcasts and radio shows focused on liberty and rights.

An example of fake news inciting anger and hatred among citizens is the 2019 Lincoln Memorial confrontation between Covington Catholic High School student Nicholas Sandmann and Native American activist Nathan Phillips. The incident was framed by mainstream media like The New York Times as an "explosive convergence of race, religion, and ideological beliefs." It was portrayed as an act of savage disrespect by students, including Sandmann, toward Phillips. Early footage and rhetoric suggested Sandmann -who was wearing a Make America Great Again (MAGA) hat- was taunting Phillips with other students encircling him, igniting widespread outrage and calls for condemnation. The outrage caused Sandmann's personal information to be released, leading to him receiving death threats. However, extended video footage later revealed that the encounter had been significantly misrepresented and that Sandmann was only standing there smiling as Phillips walked up and got in his face while chanting. This case shows how selective reporting and sophist rhetoric by mainstream media and government can fuel division and purposely exacerbate social tensions.

A striking example of how government and powerful entities influence mainstream media rhetoric is videos showing local news stations across the U.S. delivering identical stories -word for word- which can only happen if a single source controls each station. In one widely circulated clip, dozens of news anchors from different stations recited the same script about the dangers of "fake news," creating a chilling display of uniformity that blurred the line between independent journalism and coordinated propaganda, which is eerily similar to the contents in George Orwell's book, *1984*. This synchronization illustrates the significant role of mainstream media in determining public rhetoric, further demonstrating how disinformation and manipulation permeate modern information channels and drive public views and desires to align with specific agendas.

Mass Psychosis

Mass psychosis is used to steer populations into irrational, fear-driven states. By exploiting fear, confusion, and propaganda, this type of PSYOP campaign creates an environment where individuals abandon critical thinking in favor of group conformity. This collective comfort in fear-driven hysteria is a powerful force. The COVID19 pandemic is a compelling example of mass psychosis in action, shaping the perception and rhetoric of society. Throughout the pandemic, government censorship, misinformation campaigns, and social ostracism played a pivotal role in driving mass psychosis, particularly around vaccination statuses and mask usage in businesses and public spaces, stressing the need for critical thinking and skepticism in all situations.

Mass psychosis as a form of psychological warfare functions as terrorism, inflicting emotional and psychological harm to destabilize societies. Fear-inducing stimuli -alarming rhetoric about pandemics, economic collapse, or geopolitical crises- are disseminated through media and social networks to keep populations in a perpetual state of anxiety and fear, rendering them more susceptible to manipulation and control. A key feature is its ability to divide and conquer. By nurturing paranoia and mistrust, these campaigns fracture societal cohesion, driving individuals toward polarizing ideologies or authoritarian figures promising security and protection. The resulting fragmentation weakens collective resistance and shifts the focus from rational discourse to emotional survival. In this state, dissent is self-policed, as individuals fear ostracism for challenging the prevailing rhetoric, leading to compliant obedience. This feedback loop amplifies conformity, enabling the objectives of the PSYOP campaign without requiring overt coercion.

As a form of psychological terrorism, mass psychosis leaves deep scars on the psyche of individuals and societies. Beyond achieving immediate strategic goals, its long-term impact includes weakened mental health and diminished capacity for critical thinking, further reinforcing the effects of manipulation and control. Recognizing this tactic is crucial to resisting manipulation and developing resilience in psychological warfare.

Limited Hangout

A limited hangout, a deceptive tactic, strategically releases partial truths or selective disclosures -a form of perception management. This method is designed to divert attention and conceal the full extent of a situation, serving to deflect scrutiny, pacify dissent, or maintain credibility while keeping critical details hidden. Governments and organizations use limited hangouts to appear transparent, preemptively releasing information to control the rhetoric and avoid deeper investigations. This can also be done by creating or infiltrating controlled opposition into movements and organizations as prominent voices, deliberately releasing limited information to appear on followers' side but ultimately leading them to the opposite of what they seek and desire.

"A 'limited hangout' is spy jargon for a favorite and frequently used gimmick of the clandestine professionals. When their veil of secrecy is shredded and they can no longer rely on a phony cover story to misinform the public, they resort to admitting—sometimes even volunteering—some of the truth while still managing to withhold the key

and damaging facts in the case. The public, however, is usually so intrigued by the new information that it never thinks to pursue the matter further." – Victor Marchetti (Special Assistant to the Deputy Director of CIA), *CIA to 'Admit' Hunt Involvement in Kennedy Slaying* (August 14th, 1978)

Controlled Opposition

Governments and other powerful entities employ controlled opposition to create or infiltrate movements and organizations. Its purpose is to misdirect opposition and disobedience, uphold the existing power structure, and divert power and momentum away from the original goal and target. Governments, in particular, can monitor and manipulate opposition movements by positioning a seemingly adversarial voice, ensuring that opposition remains contained and non-threatening. Individuals operating as controlled opposition do not need to know they are functioning as one.

Intelligence agencies use controlled opposition by funding or influencing activist groups to steer them toward less effective or divisive tactics. Controlled opposition dilutes genuine resistance by co-opting leadership or framing the opposition as extreme or illegitimate, discouraging broader public support. This tactic ensures that dissent remains a manageable force. All political parties and movements that might threaten government control are co-opted so they can be managed.

For example, during the 2024 Presidential Election, prominent "leadership" members of the Libertarian Party (LP) began to advocate for President Trump, Elon Musk, and Robert F. Kennedy Jr. (RFK Jr), distancing themselves from the actual LP nominee, Chase Oliver. This was a crucial time for the party, as it was an opportunity to present a united front and promote their nominee. However, Libertarian National Committee (LNC) Chair Angela McArdle went so far as to support replacing Oliver with RFK Jr on some state ballets. Regardless of the views on Oliver as the LP nominee pick, advocating for the others who have been historically not libertarian is suspicious and should be questioned in detail.

It's essential to question motives, as later, it was discovered that several RFK Jr organizations filtered close to $800,000 through McArdle's organizations, with $25,000 earmarked for her organization with additional amounts being given to her spouse. In return, McArdle advocated for and supported a joint fundraiser between RFK Jr's campaign and the LP. In addition, the LP officially sent out an email for the joint fundraiser with donations to one of McArdle's organizations, which received over $450,000. Afterward, McArdle promoted RFK Jr as a libertarian and President Trump's campaign as the path toward freedom and a way to get libertarians into high-level government rulership positions with a few other supposed "promises." McArdle failed to disclose this financial conflict of interest to LP members, highlighting a significant lack of transparency in the party's leadership. RFK Jr's policies and views do not align with libertarian principles. The argument and public discourse as to why RFK Jr is a "libertarian" is due to him paying for the lifetime LP membership dues -name over actions and principles.

Another possible example from within the libertarian and anarchist communities is when Liberty Hangout, a proclaimed anarcho-capitalist alternative media organization -now sounds like limited hangout and controlled opposition- started to advocate for President Trump in 2016 when he was anything but a libertarian and anarchist. Following "Statist" Hangout's path, the libertarian alternative media organization Being Libertarian started advocating for President Trump's campaign in 2024, making it seem more like Being "Statist." **Do these incidents and examples sound like limited hangouts and controlled opposition?**

In my previous book on COVID19, I detailed my reasons for believing that figures such as President Trump, President Biden, Elon Musk, and talk show host Tucker Carlson play roles of controlled opposition. They are in positions to conduct limited hangouts to keep people pacified or to get them angry with a limited specific focus. My opinion remains unchanged after observing developments over the two years since the book was published. Considering the scope and details within this book, everyone must engage in critical thinking and ask questions at every step and action of anyone being presented as a savior and defeater of the "Deep State" government. I will only go into brief details about President Trump due to winning the 2024 Presidential Election and being in power for four more years. Still, I know there are connections and evidence to suggest controlled opposition for each of the above names and many more.

President Trump presents a compelling case for being controlled opposition. His actions and history contradict the anti-establishment and libertarian rhetoric he championed during his 2016, 2020, and 2024 campaigns. Before running as a Republican for the 2016 presidential race -switched parties on July 16th, 2015- he had a long history as a Democrat, raising questions about his ideological consistency. This is the first potential indication of controlled opposition. Despite campaigning as a pro-Second Amendment advocate, President Trump signed more gun control measures into law than President Obama or President Biden. His 2018 bump stock ban, established through executive order, was later ruled unconstitutional. He also made the controversial statement in 2018, "Take the guns first, go through due process second," which are unconstitutional violations of the Second and Fifth Amendments. His family's historical ties to Israel and his outspoken support for its government further align him with establishment geopolitics.

Under President Trump's administration, Operation Warp Speed fast-tracked the development of mRNA COVID19 vaccines, funneling billions of taxpayer dollars into pharmaceutical corporations with questionable safety oversight and legislatively approved liability protections for manufacturers. He also signed the CARES Act into law in March 2020, a COVID19 relief bill that orchestrated the most significant transfer of wealth in human history, disproportionately benefiting corporations and the elite while leaving much of the working class to struggle. The bill's provisions and subsequent Federal Reserve policies led to the borrowing of newly created dollars, injecting significant inflation into the economy and devaluing the U.S. dollar. This, in turn, worsened conditions for the poor and middle class, further devaluing the dollar's purchasing power while causing the national debt to spike by $4 trillion by the end of 2020, with the actual total after several years incalculable.

President Trump's rhetoric and specific actions have painted him as a champion of anti-establishment ideals and in defiance of globalist agendas, but his other policies suggest controlled opposition. For example, President Trump announced the creation of an External Revenue Service (ERS) for imposed tariffs and his desire to incorporate Greenland, Canada, and Mexico into the U.S., further moving toward globalist agendas. If he were controlled opposition, strategically opposing specific aspects of the United Nations (U.N.) and World Economic Forum's (WEF) Agenda 2030 would have bolstered his image among his voter base while pushing this agenda in other ways.

For example, in June 2017, President Trump announced the U.S. withdrawal from the Paris Agreement, a global accord aimed at combating climate change and a key component of the U.N.'s Sustainable Development Goals (SDGs). This decision, formalized on November 4th, 2020, along with his administration's rollback of numerous environmental regulations and promotion of fossil fuel development, diverged from the environmental sustainability objectives outlined in Agenda 2030. At the same time, his Operation Warp Speed and global vaccine distribution efforts were pivotal in laying the foundation for centralized control aligned with the Agenda 2030 goals. He also pledged $4 billion in taxpayer funds to the Global Alliance for Vaccines and Immunization (GAVI) -a Bill and Melinda Gates Foundation initiative- to distribute mRNA vaccines globally. These efforts facilitated unprecedented collaboration between governments, pharmaceutical corporations, and international organizations, integrating health strategies into broader aspects of surveillance and compliance within Agenda 2030.

President Trump's administration emphasized "America First" in vaccine distribution; however, early participation in global vaccine distribution and data-sharing initiatives paved the way for centralized control and alignment with Agenda 2030 goals. Analyzing President Trump's record and history holistically suggests that his presidency may have placated dissenting voices opposing a growing tyrannical government while advancing policies that enriched and empowered the elites he ostensibly opposed.

"I could stand in the middle of Fifth Avenue and shoot somebody, and I wouldn't lose any voters, okay? It's, like, incredible." – President Donald Trump, *Campaign Rally Sioux Center, Iowa* (January 23rd, 2016)

Co-Optation

Co-optation is a psychological and social technique where governments, organizations, or individuals infiltrate and redirect grassroots movements to serve their agendas. This tactic allows for manipulating movements that might otherwise threaten the status quo or provide protection and benefit to specific individuals. For example, the "Woke" movements, incorporating multiple movements like Occupy Wall Street and Black Lives Matter over the years, initially aimed to raise awareness of social justice issues and the mechanisms behind them. However, corporate interests and government and political forces co-opted these movements, typically through agent provocateurs, quickly turning them into negative connotations, causing harm instead of the awareness they set out to raise. The phrase "Go Woke, Go Broke" emerged as businesses adopting superficial woke messaging for public relations purposes faced backlash for perceived inauthenticity, alienating customers, and showing a desire to pander to a small group of disenfranchised individuals at the expense of a larger customer base. This demonstrates how co-optation can dilute the original intent of a movement, rendering it ineffective or counterproductive.

Another example is the LGBTQA+ movement, which began as a push for equal rights and acceptance of diverse sexual orientations - LGB. Initially centered on combating discrimination and celebrating being comfortable in your skin, it expanded to include gender identity issues and more. While inclusivity is vital, the '+' symbol opened the door for other groups, including pedophiles, to attempt to reframe their actions as socially acceptable and cause for celebration under the phrase "minor-attracted persons." This hijacking caused internal divisions and damaged public support, diminishing the movement's original mission due to the rhetoric introduced by these co-opted elements. However, groups like *Gays Against Groomers* have risen in response, actively fighting against the infiltration and attempting to reclaim the movement's integrity. These groups play a crucial role in the fight against co-optation, aiming to preserve the original mission of promoting equal rights and acceptance of decisions between consenting adults while firmly opposing attempts to normalize harmful and disgusting behaviors that violate the rights of children. Co-optation turns genuine movements into tools for distraction, division, and control.

These examples are hallmark signs of past government operations like COINTELPRO, which was a counterintelligence program between 1956 and 1971 that was used to infiltrate, surveil, discredit, and subvert various organizations and individuals that were gaining power and influence. COINTELPRO was used to undermine the feminist movement, the Communist Party of the USA, Martin Luther King Jr., the Nation of Islam, the Black Panther Party, and many more organizations and individuals. COINTELPRO used the full scope of PSYOPs, including violence and assassinations, to achieve its goals of "protecting national security and political order." Even though the official COINTELPRO program ended, the practices and goals continue to affect society today through other named and unnamed programs.

Censorship

Government censorship stifles dissenting voices and shapes rhetoric in favor of government interests. The suppression of speech, public communication, or other information becomes particularly alarming when governments collaborate with social media corporations to remove content, a clear violation of the First Amendment. This partnership has silenced accounts and voices that challenge government-approved rhetoric, including the censorship of information that later proved to be factual, often through government-influenced "Fact Checkers." My social media accounts have been highly censored due to posting about the research I've conducted and what is found in my published works.

Through legislation, regulatory bodies, and direct intervention, governments suppress information that challenges authority or exposes inconvenient truths. This practice significantly hampers public discourse, restricts access to diverse perspectives, and fosters an environment where only government-approved rhetoric prevails. Censorship is no longer only a book-burning action and can be harder to detect and defend against.

High-profile examples of censorship, such as the suppression of whistleblowers, banning controversial figures from digital platforms, or the direct removal of content, serve as harsh reminders of how censorship can shape public perception and action. By controlling the flow of information, governments can steer rhetoric, quell opposition and disobedience, and bolster centralized power at the expense of transparency, accountability, and the Right to Free Speech.

Deepfakes

Deepfakes, computer-generated "fake" videos, images, or audio recordings, are a new tool governments and intelligence entities use to deceive the public. They can depict anyone doing or saying anything, from fabricated political speeches to staged events in foreign countries, and can convince society that something false is true. With the advancement of AI, deepfakes are becoming easier to create and spread to unsuspecting individuals. The rise of deepfakes has added a new, alarming dimension to psychological manipulation, calling into question the confidence in visual and auditory evidence. It's crucial to be skeptical and critical when encountering such content.

Sock puppet Accounts

Sockpuppet accounts are fake online personas created to engage with real users, spread propaganda, and amplify rhetoric that aligns with specific objectives, making it seem like the masses favor one side of an issue over another. These accounts are operated by government agents or private contractors and are designed to appear authentic, complete with fabricated backstories, history, and social connections. Initially developed by U.S. Central Command, programs like Operation Earnest Voice allowed agents to create and manage sockpuppet accounts to influence foreign and domestic targets on social media platforms. Sockpuppet accounts are a direct extension of government-sponsored disinformation and misinformation campaigns, creating an echo chamber that normalizes propaganda and suppresses opposition. These operations and campaigns have been used for several decades.

"*War is peace. Freedom is slavery. Ignorance is strength.*" – George Orwell, *1984* (1984)

Historical Examples

Operation Mockingbird

Initiated by the Central Intelligence Agency (CIA) in 1948, Operation Mockingbird demonstrates the use of mainstream media as a tool for psychological influence. This program aimed to recruit journalists and media outlets to disseminate pro-American propaganda during the Cold War. By embedding CIA-approved rhetoric in mainstream news, the operation shaped public opinion both domestically and internationally. It allowed the government to subtly manipulate foreign policy perceptions and promote support for U.S. actions while stifling dissent. The program's covert nature raises ethical concerns about media independence and the rights of citizens to access unbiased information. The long-term effects of Operation Mockingbird continue to shape our media landscape and public perception today, with these types of operations and campaigns growing more efficient and effective over time.

Star Wars

The Strategic Defense Initiative (SDI), famously nicknamed the "Star Wars" program, was announced by President Ronald Reagan in 1983. This cutting-edge missile defense system would be capable of intercepting nuclear missiles in space and proposed the development of advanced technologies such as space-based lasers, particle beam weapons, and ground-based interceptors to shield the U.S. from nuclear attacks. While publicly framed as a genuine defense initiative, SDI functioned effectively as a PSYOP aimed at the Union of Soviet Socialist Republics (USSR) during the Cold War.

The announcement of SDI, leveraging the fear of technological inferiority, put pressure on the USSR to pour vast resources into countering a system that never materialized. The U.S. never came close to building or deploying most of the technologies proposed under SDI, as they were largely aspirational and faced insurmountable technical challenges. However, the perception of SDI as an imminent game-changer intensified the USSR's economic decline, as it diverted critical resources into military and space programs. The Star Wars program is a prime example of how strategic misinformation and psychological manipulation can achieve geopolitical objectives without technological implementation.

QAnon: A Speculative PSYOPs

QAnon is most likely a striking example of a PSYOP campaign designed to manipulate perceptions, cultivate groupthink, and influence behavior. Emerging in late 2017, QAnon centered around 4chan cryptic messages of "Q," an anonymous figure claiming insider knowledge of a secret war between good and evil factions within the U.S. government. Followers of Q were encouraged to "trust the plan" and await the dismantling of a so-called "Deep State" by a shadowy group of patriots working to protect President Trump from another "Deep State" shadowy group. While this rhetoric resonated deeply with disillusioned individuals seeking justice and transparency, it bore all the hallmarks of a sophisticated intelligence campaign.

At the heart of QAnon's success were mechanisms typical of PSYOPs: disinformation, emotional manipulation, and the cultivation of dependency through hope and fear. Q's cryptic messages rarely offered concrete evidence, relying instead on vague predictions that followers interpreted to fit current events. This ambiguity allowed rhetoric to persist even as predictions consistently failed to materialize. The emotional manipulation was potent -followers were fueled by hope that justice was imminent and by fear of an all-powerful cabal threatening their way of life. Combined with a sense of community and a call to "decode" Q's messages, QAnon used an echo chamber of belief and groupthink, where dissent was silenced, to further ensnare followers with rhetoric that kept them docile.

For example, "The Storm" was a prediction that a massive media blackout would take place on March 4th, 2021, and August 13th, 2021, where pedophiles within the government and "Deep State" operatives would be arrested and that President Trump would be reinstated as the rightful president over President Biden. This prediction failed to occur, but its true purpose was successful -keeping individuals thinking someone would save them from the tyranny being implemented within the government.

Adding credibility to QAnon's rhetoric, President Trump made references that seemed to endorse the movement, such as retweeting Q-related content or responding positively to Q-related phrases during rallies. These gestures gave QAnon immense validation among President Trump's cult base, further entwining the movement with his presidency. Even though the core promises of QAnon -that a shadowy group of insiders within the government would take down the Deep State- never came to fruition, most ignored the obvious and continued to put faith in this entity. Instead of critically thinking, followers were repeatedly told to wait, reinforcing passivity and deterring any meaningful action against perceived tyranny. This focus on "trust the plan" is a key feature of PSYOPs, redirecting potential activism into inertia while maintaining control over the rhetoric.

Some speculation points to organizations like In-Q-Tel, the CIA's venture capital arm, as potential architects of QAnon, leveraging advanced technologies and methodologies to achieve psychological control over those seeking to limit government power. Its portfolio includes Palantir Technologies for data mining and behavioral prediction, Babel Street for social media analytics, and Recorded Future for predictive AI. These tools align seamlessly with the requirements of a campaign that monitors public sentiment, tailors rhetoric, and adjusts strategies in real-time. Using PSYOPs with these systems and tools provides a dangerous combination of unethical and immoral capabilities in the government's hands.

Ultimately, QAnon may have been an elaborate PSYOP aimed at sowing division, cultivating blind obedience, and directing public opposition into ineffective channels. Its repeated failure to deliver on promises, reliance on emotional manipulation, and seeming alignment with advanced intelligence technologies suggest it was more than a grassroots movement. Whether designed to appease President Trump's followers, distract from real issues, or achieve other objectives, QAnon is a powerful case study of how PSYOPs can operate in the digital age. While the whole truth may never be known, QAnon reminds us of the critical need for vigilance, critical thinking, and skepticism in a world increasingly shaped by psychological warfare.

PSYOPs have evolved into a holistically interconnected ecosystem spanning all countries and governments, driving everyone toward an increasingly authoritarian surveillance state aligned with the U.N. and WEF's Agenda 2030. A. This monstrous apparatus, encompassing governments, intelligence agencies, corporations, academic institutions, and advanced technological tools, wields immense power in shaping public rhetoric, controlling dissenting voices, and consolidating authority. Efforts promoting literacy and critical thinking are critical, but when through government-approved efforts, they are inadequate against modern manipulation tactics' sheer scale and sophistication.

Intelligence agencies like the CIA, NSA, and FBI maintain specialized divisions focused on psychological manipulation. These groups operate covertly, conducting missions with minimal oversight and answering only to a few unelected officials. This doesn't account for the numerous government-sanctioned and unsanctioned unnamed groups and entities acting globally with impunity. Additionally, partnerships between intelligence agencies and academic institutions ensure a steady flow of trained operatives for government and corporate

PSYOP campaigns. For example, the Department of War Studies at King's College London has been linked to Western intelligence agencies, training analysts, journalists, social media managers, and fact-checkers to take up roles within social media platforms. Many graduates of such programs hold influential positions at major corporations, including Google, Meta, X, and TikTok, where they shape public discourse under content moderation and fact-checking.

On a global scale, intelligence entities and programs focused on PSYOPs have seen a surge in training operatives in the latest techniques for psychological manipulation. These organizations teach various methods, from limited hangouts to deepfakes to manufactured cultural and social rhetoric in the form of propaganda. Israel's Cyber-Intelligence Division, IDF Unit 8200, is a prime example of merging intelligence training and corporate influence. Hundreds of former Unit 8200 agents have taken up paramount cybersecurity and AI positions for big tech corporations like Microsoft, Google, Meta, and X, where they continue to apply their expertise in data collection and psychological manipulation. This raises the question, **are these individuals innocent people working at what they do best, or are they also serving a grander purpose through manipulation and surveillance?**

Whistleblowers like Edward Snowden have revealed the extensive scope of mass surveillance, yet the systems they expose remain largely unaccountable. To make matters worse, **was Snowden's release of information a limited hangout distracting everyone from the still-hidden tools and capabilities?**

The lack of robust legal frameworks or independent oversight aggravates the issue, as technological advancements in AI and data analytics enable unprecedented levels of disinformation and behavior control. Everyone plays a crucial role in combating PSYOPs; however, most are not even aware of the PSYOPs to keep pace with the innovation of those engineering the manipulation. As with chess, decisions and actions are being thought of and planned 15+ moves ahead. **Do you see the government stopping this apparatus from being forced upon us?**

Without a significant concerted effort, modern PSYOPs will continue to pave the way to peak Tyranny, where surveillance, manipulation, and disinformation are not just tools of control but the foundational structure of governance and truth.

"And if all others accepted the lie which the Party imposed -if all records told the same tale — then the lie passed into history and became truth. Who controls the past,' ran the Party slogan, 'controls the future: who controls the present controls the past. And yet the past, though of its nature alterable, never had been altered. Whatever was true now was true from everlasting to everlasting. It was quite simple. All that was needed was an unending series of victories over your own memory. 'Reality control', they called it: in Newspeak, 'doublethink'." – George Orwell, *1984* (1984)

Conspiracy Theories

"For we are opposed around the world by a monolithic and ruthless conspiracy that relies primarily on covert means for expanding its sphere of influence--on infiltration instead of invasion, on subversion instead of elections, on intimidation instead of free choice, on guerrillas by night instead of armies by day. It is a system which has conscripted vast human and material resources into the building of a tightly knit, highly efficient machine that combines military, diplomatic, intelligence, economic, scientific and political operations. Its preparations are concealed, not published. Its mistakes are buried, not headlined. Its dissenters are silenced, not praised. No expenditure is questioned, no rumor is printed, no secret is revealed. It conducts the Cold War, in short, with a war-time discipline no democracy would ever hope or wish to match." – John F. Kennedy, *The President and the Press* (April 27th, 1961)

The concept of conspiracy theories, deeply rooted in history, is a fascinating subject that has intrigued scholars and historians for centuries. Evidence of such ideas can be traced back to ancient Greece's political and social contexts and beyond. In the fifth century BCE, the Athenian statesman and historian Thucydides documented examples of political intrigue and suspicion during the Peloponnesian War, where factions believed rivals were conspiring to seize power. Similarly, ancient Roman politics was rife with accusations of conspiracies, such as the infamous plot by Brutus and others to assassinate Julius Caesar in 44 BCE. These early examples reveal that conspiracy theories -beliefs that covert groups orchestrate events to achieve hidden agendas- have long been a part of human societies.

'**Conspiracy theory**' is *a point of view that a group is plotting something sinister -often in secret- using direct movements and actions to control what is being seen, like in the sense of theater.*

The previous examples further support this definition. At its core, it involves the crucial role of questioning the rhetoric presented by those in positions of authority. This active questioning seeks to uncover hidden motives and agendas, empowering us to take responsibility for our understanding of the truth. While not every conspiracy theory is accurate or factual, dismissing them outright ignores the reality that conspiracies exist -so much so that there are formal conspiracy laws at both federal and state levels. These laws acknowledge that individuals and groups can collaborate covertly to achieve unethical, immoral, and illegal goals. **If conspiracy theories never existed, how did the phrase come into existence?**

The term 'conspiracy theory' itself has been weaponized as part of PSYOPs to discredit dissenting views and opinions and shield government actions from scrutiny. In 1967, the CIA deliberately sought to attach a negative connotation to the term. The campaign, detailed in the now-declassified document *Countering Criticism of the Warren Report*, was specifically designed to disrupt public skepticism surrounding the assassination of President John F. Kennedy (JFK). By labeling dissenters of the government-approved rhetoric as "conspiracy theorists," the CIA effectively shifted attention away from the substantive flaws in the Warren Report, discrediting opposing voices without addressing their claims. Mainstream media plays a crucial role in perpetuating or debunking conspiracy theories, often amplifying them for sensationalism or debunking them through sophist means, enabling the dismissal of uncomfortable truths as mere paranoia.

This calculated effort to stigmatize the term 'conspiracy theory' serves as a potent example of how governments employ PSYOPs to maintain control using the alteration of language and communication. The government demands compliance and discourages independent thought by framing those who question government-approved rhetoric as irrational, untrustworthy, and domestic terrorists. The phenomenon suppresses legitimate inquiry, making it easier for those in power to consolidate more power and impose their will cloaked in the appearance of protecting society. When viewed in this light, the dismissal of conspiracy theories becomes another aspect of Tyranny, silencing dissent and insulating government actions from accountability.

Voting Fraud

The integrity of elections has long been considered an essential aspect of a government *-for the people, by the people*. However, allegations of voting fraud and electoral manipulation have challenged citizens' confidence in these systems during nearly every election. High-profile claims of electoral fraud have arisen in pivotal moments, such as the contentious *Bush v. Gore* decision in 2000, which centered on disputed ballots in Florida, and accusations of Russian interference in the 2016 election. Similarly, the 2020 presidential election faced widespread fraud claims, including debates over mail-in ballots, electronic voting systems, and irregularities in vote counting. These recurring allegations show the fragile state of electoral confidence and the perception that the democratic process is vulnerable to internal and external manipulation, which, left unchecked, leads to widespread oppression. It's essential to be aware of these historical examples to understand the challenges to electoral integrity. Interestingly is that those who pushed voting fraud in 2020 when President Trump lost consider the 2024 election to be above board -no voting fraud- because President Trump won, not realizing that the most likely truth is that he was selected to win. The fraud still took place but in a different manner.

The potential for electoral fraud is a serious concern that should raise alarm about the integrity of the U.S. election process. Governments and powerful entities are willing to commit fraud to ensure the election of pre-selected candidates -controlled opposition- invalidating an election's integrity. From internal party politics to vulnerabilities in electronic voting systems, the potential for undermining the voting process is ever-present. Cases like the Republican National Committee's (RNC) sabotage of Ron Paul's campaign in 2012, the Democratic National Committee's (DNC) sabotage of Bernie Sanders' campaign in 2016, and ongoing controversies surrounding non-citizen voting and foreign influence should call the state of electoral transparency and validity into question.

RNC 2012

In 2012, allegations surfaced that the RNC -Republican Party- manipulated the primary nomination process to sideline Ron Paul, a candidate with significant grassroots support who should have won the nominee. Reports of rule changes, delegate manipulation, fraud, and procedural irregularities leading up to and at the Republican National Convention in Tampa, Florida, depicted a corrupt private organization prioritizing establishment candidates, with glaring questions and red flags over the apparent nominee. These actions were viewed by many as a deliberate effort to suppress an anti-establishment voice in favor of candidates more aligned with party leadership and deeper agendas. The incident left a lasting skepticism about whether internal party politics subverts voter choice in support of a system prioritizing controlled opposition over genuine democracy, further indicating the devaluing of individuals' voting power before the election.

DNC 2016

In 2016, the DNC -Democratic Party- faced significant backlash when leaked emails and documents were released by an anonymous source, Guccifer 2.0, through Wikileaks, suggesting collusion to favor Hillary Clinton over Bernie Sanders during the primary nomination. The leaked emails and documents revealed a concentrated effort to undermine Sanders' campaign, calling into question the DNC's impartiality when nominating a candidate and casting a heavy shadow over the entire election process. Interestingly, the leaked information was never claimed to be fake or misinformation, only that it was released to "interfere with democracy" by Russian hackers. Adding to the controversy, Seth Rich, the DNC Voter Expansion Data Director, was murdered under suspicious circumstances shortly after the leaks. While officially deemed a botched robbery, the circumstances of the murder -nothing was stolen, and Rich was shot in the back- spurred speculation that he might have been the source of the leaks, not Russian hackers as widely claimed by the DNC and Clinton. Guccifer 2.0 claimed that Rich was his source. Wikileaks' offered a $20,000 reward for information leading to the suspect's arrest. Additionally, Julian Assange provided cryptic remarks about the reward when interviewed, hinting that Rich was the source of the email leaks.

Regardless of personal opinions on Sanders' political stances or character, his campaign during the 2016 Democratic primary nomination process was undeniably a grassroots movement that resonated with millions, particularly among younger voters and progressives. Sanders garnered significant popular support, making him the frontrunner and apparent nominee for the entire race. However, despite this momentum, the nomination was ultimately handed to Clinton, raising questions about the transparency and fairness of the DNC nomination process.

The RNC and DNC are considered private corporations -not government entities- with protected rights. In the court case ***Wilding v. DNC Services Corp.***, **No. 17-14194 (11th Cir. 2019)**, the court upheld DNC's status as a private organization with First Amendment rights, including the right to free association and control over its internal affairs

-not legally obligated to maintain neutrality. **How do we know that controlled opposition is not predetermined for us to vote on?**

Electronic Voting – Dominion, ES&S, Hart InterCivic

The reliability of electronic voting systems, including Dominion Voting Systems, Election Systems & Software (ES&S), and Hart InterCivic, has long been a contentious topic, with some pointing to vulnerabilities that could weaken election integrity. In December 2019, several Democratic senators, including Elizabeth Warren, Amy Klobuchar, and Ron Wyden, sent letters raising serious concerns about these companies' security, ownership, and transparency, which collectively manage a significant portion of the U.S. voting infrastructure. The senators highlighted the lack of accountability and secrecy surrounding the companies' corporate structures, raising questions about potential risks to election integrity due to ownership consolidation and insufficient cybersecurity measures. They stressed the need to disclose ownership details and cybersecurity protocols. However, the responses from the companies were not made public, and little information has surfaced about subsequent congressional actions or follow-ups, leaving these critical concerns unanswered.

By 2023, the DHS Cybersecurity and Infrastructure Security Agency (CISA) issued warnings about the potential for foreign actors to target U.S. election systems, worsening public unease. Additionally, cybersecurity experts claimed to have exposed systemic vulnerabilities in these systems, such as encryption keys stored in plain text, unauthorized access, and changes made without detection and logging, creating an environment that could not produce audit trails. Despite these alarming revelations, the Supreme Court declined to hear related court cases providing the evidence, leaving significant questions about the integrity and security of electronic voting systems unanswered. The ongoing lack of transparency and accountability surrounding these voting technology companies continues to fuel debates about the vulnerabilities of modern electoral processes and their implications for democracy. The potential for this process of altering and controlling an election outcome to transition from Democracy to Tyranny is a grave concern that should not be ignored.

Non-Citizens

Non-citizen voting has become a hot topic, raising concerns about the trustworthiness of election results and the equitable value of each citizen's vote. When non-citizens participate in elections, they alter the outcome by introducing an unknown number of potential votes, diluting the influence and pool of legitimate voters. This dilution sabotages the principle of *"one person, one vote"* and creates disparities in representation that may not reflect the citizenry's will. Moreover, including non-citizen votes disproportionately affects tightly contested races, where even a few unqualified votes can alter the results. This diminishes the electoral power of citizen voters and drives significant questions about the trustworthiness of the democratic process, potentially leading to a crisis of legitimacy.

Mass government-sanctioned migrations further complicate the issue by introducing systemic challenges to electoral integrity and resource allocation. Policies encouraging large-scale migration strain social services and impact employment markets. The shift in demographic trends influences political outcomes. When governments facilitate such migration, prioritizing globalist objectives over the welfare of existing citizens, they destabilize communities and diminish any semblance of voting power from citizens. This strategy creates voting blocs dependent on government programs, swaying elections in favor of those who endorse such policies, entrenching political power and control, and marginalizing the voices of existing citizens.

For example, in 2024, the U.S. approved a $95 billion military aid package directed toward Ukraine, Israel, and Taiwan. Within this package, $481 million was allocated specifically for mass migration centers to facilitate the relocation of Middle Eastern immigrants to U.S. cities. Unrelated to military aid, this allocation raises questions about the intertwining of foreign aid and mass migration policies. These policies strain local resources and are strategically designed to destabilize the regions, reduce citizens' voting power, and shift the demographic and political landscapes. These actions reinforce suspicions of the government prioritizing globalist agendas over the needs and rights of its citizens, continuing the progression toward Tyranny.

Foreign Influence

Foreign interference in U.S. elections has been an ongoing issue that is brought up during each election, with the 2016 Russian election interference rhetoric standing out as a prominent example. The widely publicized claims suggested that Russian operatives sought to influence the election outcome through disinformation campaigns and cyber activities, such as alleged hacking and the release of emails and documents from DNC servers. Subsequent investigations cast doubt on key aspects of these Russian interference claims, with the rhetoric increasingly viewed as a politically motivated hoax and disinformation campaign used to delegitimize the leaked information. Beyond Russia, examples of Chinese and Israeli influence have surfaced in recent years. For decades, China and Israel have been accused of using economic leverage and disinformation campaigns to shape U.S. policies and influence politicians. For example, intelligence reports have shown efforts by Chinese operatives to forge relationships and acquire leverage over lawmakers to gain policy influence.

Similarly, Israel's influence in U.S. politics is criticized for its far-reaching implications on lawmakers and policy-making. The American Israel Public Affairs Committee (AIPAC) is one of the most powerful lobbying organizations in the U.S., channeling significant resources to influence members of Congress to adopt pro-Israel stances. AIPAC routinely organizes high-profile conferences attended by top U.S. lawmakers and funds political campaigns of candidates who align with its agenda. The result is a striking bipartisan commitment to military aid and foreign policies that favor Israel, even when they may conflict with broader U.S. or global interests. Additionally, many politicians and those in high-level positions throughout various industries have strong ties to Israel, further influencing the election process in favor of Israel.

For example, the U.S. provides billions of taxpayer dollars in military aid and support to Israel annually due to legislation being heavily influenced by pro-Israel lobbying, driving the full backing of most politicians in Congress. Many politicians fly the Israel flag with the U.S. flag, showing their support and dedication to the foreign country. This display of foreign patriotism is a sign of influences that compromise the impartiality of U.S. foreign policy, particularly in the Middle East. High-profile cases, such as the involvement of individuals with dual U.S.-Israeli citizenship in policy advisory roles and the widespread bipartisan support for policies like the anti-BDS (Boycott, Divestment, Sanctions) legislation, demonstrate Israel's impact on U.S. actions domestically and internationally. The entrenched nature of Israel's influence shows how foreign actors can shape domestic political landscapes, even in the U.S., leaving voters unaware of the extent to which external interests sway their politicians.

While foreign influence in U.S. elections garners significant attention, the U.S. has a long and impactful history of interfering in elections worldwide to maintain global dominance. From orchestrating coups to funding opposition parties, the U.S. has shaped electoral outcomes to align with its strategic interests for many decades. Examples include the CIA's involvement in the 1953 Iranian coup to secure oil interests and the 1973 Chilean coup that overthrew democratically elected President Salvador Allende. More recently, the U.S. has been accused of influencing elections in Venezuela, Ukraine, and other nations through financial support for opposition groups and PSYOP media campaigns. Such actions illustrate the double standard in condemning foreign influence domestically while actively engaging in similar practices abroad. The U.S. consolidates its geopolitical power by interfering in global elections, ensuring that governments align with its economic and political agenda. This widespread manipulation violates the authority of other nations and perpetuates instability, further fueling international tensions.

Experimentation on Citizens

Throughout history, governments worldwide have demonstrated a willingness to conduct experiments on their citizens in the name of scientific progress, public health, or national security. Shrouded in secrecy and deceit, these experiments expose the dark reality of governmental overreach and disregard for individual rights. From public health initiatives turned sinister to covert operations driven by geopolitical competition, these programs reveal a disturbing pattern of ethical and moral violations and abuse of power. The following examples -spanning decades and touching countless lives- illustrate how governments have consistently crossed ethical and moral boundaries to pursue their agendas, leaving lasting scars on individuals and societies, with the effects still felt today.

Tuskegee Experiment

The Tuskegee Experiment, conducted from 1932 to 1972 by the U.S. Public Health Service, is one of the most egregious examples of unethical government experimentation. Framed as a public health study, it involved 600 black men, with 399 unknowingly infected with syphilis under the pretense of receiving free healthcare and treatment for "bad blood." The men were deliberately denied appropriate medical treatment, even after penicillin was identified as an effective cure, resulting in severe health complications and deaths, which also tragically impacted their spouses and children's health. The ongoing impact of the Tuskegee Experiment is a stark reminder of the lasting effects of such unethical practices. This blatant exploitation stresses not only the dangerous convergence of government authority and medical negligence but also the role of systemic racism in perpetuating such unethical practices.

Operation Paperclip

Following World War II, the U.S. government-initiated Operation Paperclip, a secret program that brought over 1,600 Nazi scientists, engineers, and technicians to the U.S. between 1945 and 1959. Despite their documented involvement in wartime atrocities, these individuals were integrated into critical U.S. programs, including the space race and military advancements. The operation prioritized Cold War strategic advantages over justice and accountability, allowing war criminals to escape prosecution in exchange for their expertise. This program demonstrates how governments are willing to compromise ethical standards for perceived national security benefits and power.

Operation Sea-Spray

From 1949 to 1969, the U.S. Army conducted biological warfare tests on unsuspecting citizens using the pretense of preparedness and national defense. Known as Operation Sea-Spray, one of the most infamous incidents involved releasing Serratia marcescens bacteria into the fog over San Francisco. The experiment led to a spike in hospital infections and at least one death, revealing the harmful consequences of these covert tests. Similar operations were carried out nationwide, demonstrating a reckless disregard for public health and safety. The parallels to modern practices, such as cloud seeding to manipulate weather -linked to concerns about chemical trails released from planes- raise ethical questions surrounding government-led experimentation.

In recent years, the U.S. government has significantly expanded its sky-spraying programs, with growing concerns about the scope and intent of these operations. Former CIA Director John Brennan publicly admitted to aerial spraying programs during a 2016 speech at the Council on Foreign Relations, referencing the use of stratospheric aerosol injections to combat climate change. These admissions and increased government funding for atmospheric modification research have amplified public skepticism about such initiatives' transparency and ethical implications. In 2024, Dubai demonstrated the potential risks of these programs when it used cloud seeding to enhance an incoming storm, leading to record flash flooding and multiple deaths. This tragic incident stresses the unintended consequences of weather manipulation and the ethical irresponsibility of governments engaged in such experiments. The scale and secrecy of these activities continue to raise alarms about potential health risks, environmental damage, and a lack of safety and accountability.

MKUltra

The CIA's MKUltra program, which ran from 1953 to 1973, stands as an example of the perils of unbridled governmental authority; under the direction of Sidney Gottlieb, the program set out to delve into mind control through experiments involving LSD, psychological torture, and brainwashing. Many of the subjects, including prisoners, psychiatric patients, and ordinary citizens, were unwitting participants; their consent was never sought. The program's methods inflicted enduring psychological and physical damage, and its findings were purportedly destroyed when the operation was exposed. MKUltra and similar clandestine programs serve as a grim example of the dangers of government violation of rights and the lengths to which it will go to assert dominance in espionage and psychological warfare.

When MKUltra was publicly uncovered in the 1970s, the CIA shifted its focus to similar projects under different names, such as Project MKOften, Operation Midnight, and Project Artichoke, to continue its exploration of psychological manipulation and behavioral control. These successor programs operated under the same cloak of secrecy, demonstrating the CIA's determination to advance its agenda despite the public's growing outrage and sense of injustice. These programs' continued experimentation and rebranding illustrate the efforts to obscure their true scope and evade accountability.

A particularly unsettling link to MKUltra can be found in the case of Lee Harvey Oswald, the suspected assassin of President JFK. Numerous reports and declassified documents suggest that Oswald had connections to the CIA, potentially tying him to covert operations and MKUltra-related activities. Oswald's mysterious past, including his defection to the Soviet Union and his return under unclear circumstances, fueled speculation about his role as a pawn in a larger conspiracy. These connections further drive the rhetoric of government involvement in manipulating individuals for covert objectives.

COVID19

The COVID19 pandemic has brought serious concerns about government transparency and ethical decision-making in public health policies. From conflicting information about the virus's origins to controversial mandates and experimental vaccine rollouts, governments worldwide have been accused of using the crisis as a means to expand control over populations. It can be argued that these policies prioritizing corporate interests over individual well-being and natural rights reflect an unsettling willingness to experiment on the public using engineered consent. Justified in the name of public safety, these measures have sparked debates about bypassing individual rights and the ethics of imposing untested medical solutions globally.

Through my research and work on COVID19, I have uncovered evidence suggesting that the COVID19 pandemic served as a live-fire exercise -a real-world test to stage, refine, and practice for managing a far deadlier pandemic planned for the future. This perspective aligns with statements made by former CIA Director John Brennan, who publicly stated that a future bird flu pandemic would be "the real pandemic," with a significantly higher mortality rate than COVID19. The COVID19 "chaos" gave governments unprecedented opportunities to gauge public compliance, refine emergency powers, and test mass vaccination infrastructure. These measures set a precedent for future scenarios, creating a blueprint for handling what may come next. **Do you remember the U.S. Army field hospitals that had been stood up but never saw any COVID19 patients?** It was almost like they were live-fire tests to see their response times for future events.

The notion of a bird flu pandemic, with its potential to decimate large portions of the population, raises ethical and logistical questions. COVID19 has demonstrated how fear can justify sweeping restrictions on natural rights. Suppose a bird flu pandemic with massively high mortality rates were to arise. In that case, the stage is already set for governments to implement even more stringent controls, with limited room for public disobedience. COVID19 was not merely a health crisis but a proving ground for policies and practices that may soon be deployed on a much larger and more lethal scale.

The potential for a planned bird flu pandemic becomes even more concerning when considering the revelations about U.S.-funded biological research in Ukraine. According to the Russian Defense

Ministry, areas captured in Ukraine included biological laboratories linked to Project UP-4, which reportedly focused on the bird flu virus (H5N1). The research allegedly involved studying its human mortality rate, estimated at 50%+, and tracking 145 transcontinental migratory bird patterns that could serve as vectors for spreading the virus globally. Combined with the findings from studies isolating genes that made the 1918 flu lethal and experiments demonstrating the hybridization potential of avian and human influenza strains, the evidence paints a grim picture. These programs suggest the probability of weaponizing bird flu to exploit its higher lethality and rapid spread, which would help consolidate power and control and further globalist agendas. The COVID19 pandemic has already shown how governments can leverage health crises to expand control, with a bird flu pandemic providing an opportunity to enable even more draconian measures under the pretext of public safety and welfare. This potential misuse of health crises should alarm us all and make us more attentive to the actions of our governments and those in power and influence, as it could lead to unprecedented levels of control and oppression.

On October 23rd, 2022, the Gates Foundation, WHO, and Johns Hopkins Center for Health Security conducted a pandemic tabletop exercise called *Catastrophic Contagion* at the Grand Challenges Annual Meeting in Brussels, Belgium. This simulation envisioned a deadly new contagion in 2025 named Severe Epidemic Enterovirus Respiratory Syndrome (SEERS), with a significantly higher mortality rate than COVID19, disproportionately affecting children and young people. The scenario projected 20 million global deaths, 15 million of whom were children. Notably, this same group previously organized *Event 201* in October 2019, which simulated a coronavirus pandemic shortly before COVID19 emerged, and the Nuclear Threat Initiative (NTI) monkeypox tabletop exercises closely mirrored subsequent monkeypox outbreaks. The accuracy of these past exercises raises serious questions about whether such foresight stems from predictive expertise and coincidence or foreknowledge. **Could SEERS be the bird flu pandemic that might have been planned for 2025?**

To further emphasize this point, the official Phase 1 human testing for a bird flu mRNA vaccine -*Safety and Immunogenicity Study of Self-Amplifying RNA Pandemic Influenza Vaccine in Adults* (NCT06602531), researched by Arcturus Therapeutics and funded by the Bill and Melinda Gates Foundation- started on December 12th, 2024. Five days later, on December 17th, 2024, the CDC confirmed the first severe bird flu infection in a human. This individual later died on January 7th, 2025, marking the first death in humans within the U.S. On January 17th, 2025, Moderna was awarded $590 million of taxpayer funds to develop an mRNA bird flu vaccine due to a supposed increase in human bird flu cases in the U.S. during 2024.

If you read my COVID19 book, you will read the evidence I found indicating how the COVID19 mRNA vaccine human trials were most likely driving variants and cases globally due to the mRNA vaccine recipients shedding the spike protein to others around them. If this is true, logic dictates that the new bird flu mRNA vaccines could cause the same shedding and issues, catalyzing a future bird flu pandemic and causing a self-fulfilling prophecy.

If you're eager to grasp the full extent of COVID19 and its implications as a live-fire exercise for what is potentially looming in the near future -a bird flu pandemic- then my first book, *COVID19 - SHORT PATH TO 'YOU'LL OWN NOTHING. AND YOU'LL BE HAPPY': Welcome to the new Age of Tyranny* (February 2023) is a must-read. I cover 141 published journal studies with an additional 41 references to help guide readers down the logical path the data took me and how it explains the potential and actual purposes -many- of the COVID19 pandemic.

Population Reduction

The discourse around whether governments are willing to take measures to reduce populations to maintain socio-political and economic control is profoundly unsettling, yet historical documents suggest that such strategies have indeed been considered at the highest levels of power and were actively sought. National Security Study Memorandum 200 (NSSM200), the *Kissinger Report*, was a classified document published on December 10th, 1974. Authored by Henry Kissinger and the U.S. National Security Council in collaboration with the CIA, USAID, and several federal departments, the report outlined the implications of global population growth on U.S. national security and overseas interests. It identified population growth in dozens of third-world countries as a critical threat to resource stability, food security, and geopolitical dominance, advocating for population control policies to secure U.S. influence worldwide.

The Kissinger Report explicitly argued that rapid population growth in developing nations could lead to food scarcity, resource depletion, and supply chain disruptions that would ripple through industrialized nations, threatening global stability and economic order. As a solution, the report recommended implementing population control measures in these countries, including widespread access to contraception, sterilization programs, and the promotion of smaller family units. However, recognizing the potential backlash and accusations of neocolonialism, the report emphasized the importance of introducing similar policies within the U.S. to avoid the appearance of targeting developing nations unfairly. This political maneuvering to avoid accusations of neocolonialism highlights the complex and controversial nature of global power dynamics, prompting a critical awareness of the political implications of such policies.

One notable example of domestic population control policies that align with the ethos of the Kissinger Report is the landmark Supreme Court decision in ***Roe v. Wade*, 410 U.S. 113 (1973)**. While Roe v.

Wade is framed as a case centered on individual rights and reproductive freedom, its broader societal and governmental implications cannot be ignored. By legalizing abortion, the ruling effectively provided a legal precedent for population control within the U.S. Advocates and opponents alike have pointed out how access to abortion services disproportionately impacted those in economically disadvantaged communities and minority populations, echoing the report's underlying themes of managing population growth to mitigate perceived resource and economic pressures. Although framed as a personal choice, integrating such policies into public health structures intersects with broader governmental objectives, stressing the fine line between individual rights and government interests.

The implications of the Kissinger Report and its associated policies extend beyond their specific recommendations, raising profound ethical and moral questions. These questions revolve around governmental overreach and oppression, the value placed on human life, and the balance between national security and individual rights. While framing population control as necessary for global stability, the document also revealed a willingness to treat human lives as variables in a geopolitical equation. This legacy fuels ongoing debates about the interconnection of public policy, ethics, and global power dynamics, showing governments' complex and controversial strategies to maintain dominance on the world stage. By intertwining domestic and international policies, the approach reflects a broader trend of aligning socio-political goals with calculated interventions in population dynamics.

Additional examples of population control ideas and goals can be seen in the infamous Georgia Guidestones, a giant granite monument erected in Georgia in 1980 by an anonymous group and destroyed by an explosion on July 6th, 2022 -the person responsible has still not been identified. The Georgia Guidestones controversially advocated maintaining a global population of 500 million in perpetual balance with nature, with many seeing it as a manifesto for depopulation by wealthy and secretive groups and organizations. The statements and goals inscribed in the granite align uncannily with overpopulation and climate change rhetoric, which should raise concerns that drastic measures could be proposed under the guise of public benefit and safety to achieve the goals. This mysterious monument adds to the broader rhetoric of elites leveraging resource scarcity and instability as pretexts for advocating sweeping social and economic changes.

The 2017 *Deagle Report* further amplifies these concerns and echoes the contexts and themes of depopulation. The report was published by Deagle.com, a private intelligence organization founded by Dr. Edwin Deagle, Jr., a former Army Intelligence Officer and national security expert. The report predicted a massive population decline in Western nations by or around 2025. For example, the U.S. was forecasted to shrink from 330 million to 100 million people -a 70% reduction. Though the report has largely been scrubbed from the internet and updated, archived copies continue circulating, fueling speculation about its intent and accuracy of the report. Dr. Deagle's connections to influential institutions such as the Council on Foreign Relations and the Rockefeller Foundation, where he served as Director of International Relations, further stoke suspicion of his and the report's alignment with global agendas. **Could this report indicate that an event, like a bird flu pandemic beginning in 2025, will lead to a massive population decline?**

Acts of Terrorism

The U.S. government has been involved in terrorist activities across the world, including acts of intimidation, violence, and destabilization to achieve political, economic, or strategic goals. While the term 'terrorism' today is used to describe non-state actors, opposite of its root definition -*government intimidation*- the actions of the U.S. government in supporting coups, conducting assassinations, and engaging in covert operations to influence foreign regimes demonstrate how government power can wield terror as a tool. From toppling democratically elected governments to backing militant groups that conduct terrorist actions on its behalf, the U.S. has consistently used these methods to maintain global dominance. These actions reflect the harsh reality that governments, including the U.S., can and do engage in behaviors that meet the criteria, context, and theme of terrorism.

Operation Northwoods

In 1962, the U.S. Joint Chiefs of Staff proposed Operation Northwoods, a plan to stage false flag terrorist attacks on U.S. soil to justify military action against Cuba. The proposed attacks included assassinations, bombings, and the hijacking of planes, all to be falsely attributed to the Cuban government. Although President JFK rejected the proposal, the document revealed the willingness of government officials to manipulate citizens through violence and deception. His rejection of Northwoods is cited in theories about his assassination, as he publicly opposed entrenched military and intelligence agendas. **Could an operation similar to Operation Northwoods be one of the driving forces behind the 9/11 attacks?**

9/11 (September 11th, 2001)

The September 11th, 2001, attacks, a horrific event that shook the world, is widely regarded as the deadliest act of terrorism on U.S. soil. The tragedy's sheer scale, timing, and impact have sparked questions about possible government complicity, negligence, and involvement. The day before the attacks, the DoD reported a staggering $2.4 trillion in unaccounted funds, a revelation that was quickly overshadowed by 9/11, diverting attention from one of the most significant financial accountability failures in U.S. history. The destruction of the Army's Resource Services Washington (RSW) office, which was responsible for maintaining crucial financial records and data, was conveniently obliterated during the attacks, effectively halting any investigations into the unaccounted trillions. The inability to verify financial transactions, identify discrepancies, and conduct accurate audits compounded concerns about the DoD's financial management. This financial irregularity, coupled with the destruction of these records, raises suspicions that the attack on this specific section of the Pentagon served a dual purpose -an act of terrorism that would mobilize patriotism in citizens and a convenient erasure of financial irregularities and audit trails.

Further skepticism about the events of 9/11 arises from the structural collapses of the World Trade Center (WTC) buildings. The group *Architects & Engineers for 9/11 Truth*, with over 3,500 professionals, has challenged the government-approved rhetoric, asserting that the collapses of WTC1, WTC2, and WTC7 bore hallmarks of controlled demolitions -*jet fuel can't melt steel beams*- rather than being solely caused by plane impacts or debris. Evidence to support this view is indicated by the molten metal found in the rubble of Ground Zero, which a plane crash and building collapse would have never created but would have been found if something like thermite had been used to cut the steel beams before the collapse. Additionally, removing and disposing of steel and debris from Ground Zero began shortly after the attacks as cleanup efforts began. A significant portion of the steel recovered was shipped to China and India for recycling and disposal starting in late 2001 and continuing into 2002, destroying evidence before independent investigators could thoroughly examine everything, making government investigators the only ones to review the evidence.

Notably, WTC7, which was not struck by a plane, fell in the same manner as WTC1 and WTC2, raising significant doubts about the events of that day. The rhetoric that fire and structural damage caused the WTC7 collapse fails to satisfy many experts, who point to the building's symmetrical and rapid descent as evidence of the deliberate intervention of controlled demolition. In the history of high-rise steel buildings, only three have collapsed due to plane crashes or fires, and all three happened on September 11th, 2001.

"*I remember getting a call from the fire department commander, telling me they were not sure they were going to be able to contain the fire. And I said, you know, we've had such a terrible loss of life, maybe the smartest thing to do is pull it. And they made that decision to pull, and we watched the building collapse.*" – Larry Silverstein, *America Rebuilds: A Year at Ground Zero*, PBS Documentary (September 10th, 2002)

These anomalies have fueled enduring suspicions that the 9/11 attacks were exploited -or even orchestrated- to, in part, justify sweeping policy changes that expanded government power under the appearance of combating terrorism. In the aftermath, the U.S. rapidly passed the Patriot Act, established mass surveillance programs through the NSA, and initiated prolonged military campaigns in Afghanistan and Iraq. These measures significantly altered the balance between civil rights and government control, advancing agendas of surveillance, military dominance, and domestic control. The events of 9/11 and the subsequent policy changes illustrate how moments of crisis can be weaponized to reduce freedoms, consolidate power, and deflect accountability. The unanswered questions surrounding the collapses and the Pentagon attack continue to demand transparency and fuel calls for a deeper investigation into the true motivations and consequences of that day.

Al-Qaeda, ISIS, and ISIL

Strong evidence points to the direct or indirect involvement of intelligence agencies, including the CIA, Mossad, and MI6, in creating or supporting groups like Al-Qaeda, ISIS, and ISIL to serve geopolitical objectives, creating a perpetuating external threat used to justify the consolidation of power and restriction of individual rights. These agencies have been implicated in providing financial and logistical support to these groups and training and arming their members. Leaked emails from Hillary Clinton in 2014 revealed that U.S. allies Saudi Arabia and Qatar provided financial support to ISIS, with the group's destabilizing activities conveniently justifying U.S. military interventions in those resource-rich regions. The name "ISIS," which aligns with the acronym for *Israel's Secret Intelligence Service*, also known as Mossad, has further fueled speculation about the group's connections to intelligence networks, adding complexity to its origins and operations.

One glaring example of these covert operations is Operation Timber Sycamore, a 2013 CIA initiative under the Obama administration that armed Syrian rebels to overthrow the Russian-allied Syrian government. This program, supported by Saudi Arabia and Israel, funneled resources meant for "moderate" rebels but instead reached major terrorist organizations through the black market. These actions show how terrorism can be manufactured and manipulated by government actors to advance regime changes, secure access to resources, and maintain global dominance while controlling rhetoric by pushing fear of terrorist acts being conducted on U.S. citizens.

Global Interventions Since WWII

Since World War II, the U.S. has been a dominant force in global politics, conducting bombings, assassinations, sabotage operations, coups, and regime changes in over 43 known countries. These interventions include the overthrow of democratically elected governments in Iran (1953), Chile (1973), and Guatemala (1954), with more recent examples including Libya (2011), Ukraine (2014), and Venezuela (2019). These operations were justified under "freedom" and "democracy" but led to long-term instability, human rights abuses, and economic exploitation. By employing such tactics, the U.S. has used terror to destabilize while securing and centralizing power, making it one of the most active actors in the realm of political violence. The actions outlined above reveal a consistent willingness by the U.S. government to engage in or support acts of terror to achieve its strategic aims, further showing how it fits the root definition of terrorism.

Political Assassinations

Governments have repeatedly demonstrated a willingness to assassinate political rulers to maintain power, control, and influence. The assassination of President JFK remains one of the most infamous cases of suspected government involvement in the death of a political figure. Beyond JFK, the U.S. government has been implicated in countless political assassinations worldwide, with covert operations targeting thousands of rulers and influential figures over the past century. These actions reveal a grim reality: governments resort to extreme measures, including assassination, to eliminate opposition or advance strategic objectives.

President JFK's Assassination (November 22nd, 1963)

On November 22nd, 1963, President JFK was assassinated during a presidential motorcade in Dallas, Texas. While the official rhetoric blamed Lee Harvey Oswald, a former Marine, as the would-be assassin, evidence suggests a far more complex conspiracy. Oswald was arrested shortly after the assassination, but initially for the murder of Dallas police officer J.D. Tippit, and later accused of assassinating President JFK. Before his death at the hands of nightclub owner Jack Ruby, Oswald maintained that he was a "patsy" in a broader intelligence operation.

Declassified documents that were released in 2022 reveal troubling connections between Oswald and the CIA. During his time in the Marines, Oswald was stationed at the Atsugi Naval Air Base in Japan, where the CIA was conducting MKUltra mind control experiments involving psychedelic drugs. A 1978 CIA memorandum by James Wilcott Jr., a former finance clerk, alleged that the agency recruited Oswald during this period. Additional documents indicate that Oswald was in contact with KGB and CIA agents in Mexico City just months before President JFK's assassination.

Further complicating the conspiracy, some theories point to the involvement of multiple shooters. The "back and to the left" motion of President JFK's head, captured in the Zapruder film, is a key piece of evidence that suggests a second shooter could have been on the Grassy Knoll. This motion, which indicates the direction from which the fatal shot was fired, contradicts the lone gunman theory. However, the theory of the Grassy Knoll pushed could be a limited hangout to distract from the truth. Another theory is that Secret Service agent William Greer, President JFK's driver, fired the fatal shot using a covert weapon designed to avoid detection. This theory is based on footage that appears to show Geer turning toward President JFK during the attack -a clear violation of protocols- raising an object toward President JFK before the back and left motion occurred. While these theories remain controversial, they illustrate the persistent public distrust in the lone gunman's explanation and the government's refusal to release all assassination-related documents.

President JFK's administration was marked by his vocal opposition to secret societies and covert government operations targeting U.S.

citizens, such as the proposed Operation Northwoods. His resistance to the "invisible hand" of power and alleged plans to disclose classified information, including details about extraterrestrial contact, have fueled suspicions that elements within the U.S. government orchestrated his assassination. His stance against these clandestine operations threatened the interests of powerful groups, potentially providing a motive for his elimination. Despite decades of investigations, the CIA's refusal to fully declassify documents continues to cast doubt on the government-approved rhetoric, leaving many to believe that he was eliminated to protect powerful interests.

Assassinations Over the Past Century

The U.S. government has engaged in covert operations, resulting in the assassinations of thousands of political targets worldwide. These acts have ranged from direct involvement to proxy actions carried out through allied groups or paramilitary "rebel" forces. For example, the assassination of Chilean President Salvador Allende in 1973 and the killing of Congolese Prime Minister Patrice Lumumba in 1961 were conducted by the U.S. government. These actions were justified in the name of combating communism, protecting national interests, or promoting democracy, but in reality, they frequently served corporate and geopolitical agendas. These examples stress a broader pattern of political violence, reflecting the lengths the U.S. government is willing to go to protect its interests. These operations not only compromise sovereignty and eat away at the moral credibility of the U.S. but also consolidate power and suppress opposition.

Pedophilia within Government

The notion that governments are infiltrated and influenced by pedophiles has gained traction due to the exposure of high-profile cases involving powerful and influential individuals, such as Jeffrey Epstein. Epstein's intricate connections with political elites, corporate moguls, and global influencers reveal a disturbing and disgusting practice of exploitation and manipulation. Far from being a lone actor, Epstein operated as a conduit for intelligence agencies, including Mossad, using child sex trafficking as a tool for blackmail. Hidden cameras in his properties captured compromising material on some of the world's most influential figures, creating leverage that could sway decisions at the highest levels of government and corporate power. Epstein's connections and activities epitomize how child sex trafficking has become an industrial-scale operation, supported -either directly or indirectly- by those in positions of authority. Victims' accounts and whistleblowers have confirmed the existence of incriminating videos seized by the FBI, yet no clients have been brought to justice, raising serious doubts about law enforcement's role. The lack of transparency surrounding his client list and the absence of accountability for those involved stress systemic corruption and raise critical questions about who truly holds power in society.

The circumstances surrounding Epstein's death in 2019 have only deepened the intrigue and fueled widespread speculation on what happened to him -officially ruled a suicide while in federal custody. His death occurred under highly suspicious circumstances, including the simultaneous failure of security cameras and guards reportedly asleep during his final moments. These irregularities have given rise to numerous conspiracy theories, ranging from his murder to silence him to claims that he used a body double and orchestrated an escape.

Some theorists point to the possibility of a broader cover-up, as Epstein's extensive connections to global elites -including prominent figures like Bill Gates- may have made him too dangerous to stand trial.

Epstein's ties to Gates gained public attention shortly before the COVID19 pandemic started. With Gates being heavily involved with all aspects of COVID19 and its ensuing pandemic, the focus on him could have been too much to let Epstein live. Epstein's connections sparked questions about Epstein's influence over powerful and influential individuals and entities. These revelations added fuel to long-standing concerns about Epstein's role as a facilitator for intelligence agencies and a manipulator of global power structures. Regardless of the exact truth, the unresolved questions surrounding his death emphasize the systemic failures -or deliberate obstructions- of justice, leaving the public to grapple with the unsettling reality of unaccountable power operating behind closed doors.

Epstein didn't kill himself!

The Epstein case is not an isolated example either. Historical and recent events reveal a pattern of influential individuals and organizations being implicated in child exploitation and trafficking. For example, Pizzagate -a controversial and widely dismissed conspiracy theory- remains a focal point of debate despite being labeled as "fake news" by mainstream media. Ben Swann, an independent journalist, investigated the leaked Podesta emails that allegedly tied prominent figures to a child trafficking ring. Swann's reporting was swiftly suppressed, causing his investigative company to be taken down, showing the lengths powerful entities will go to silence questions that could uncover evidence and truth. Meanwhile, revelations, and far from the only one, such as the arrest of Rahamim Shy, an Obama-era senior advisor, for child sex offenses continue to fuel concerns about systemic abuse among those in the highest echelons of government.

Beyond Epstein and the Pizzagate incident, numerous cases involving politicians from both major U.S. political parties further validate concerns about pedophiles operating within the government. From high-profile figures like Anthony Weiner to lesser-known cases involving state representatives and local officials, the repeated exposure of child sex and exploitation crimes committed by elected rulers cannot be dismissed as mere coincidence.

Additionally, in 2024, President Trump -who was friends with Epstein- nominated Matt Gaetz as his first pick for Attorney General, who quickly withdrew his nomination due to a House Ethics Committee report being prepared to be released. When the report was released, it detailed illegal activities by Gaetz, including paying to have sex with a minor, which falls under state and federal statutory rape laws. Gaetz was friends with and went to organized parties by Joel Greenberg -in prison for sex trafficking of a minor. Greenberg was a close friend and associate of Leslie Wexner -an Epstein client and founder of Victoria's Secret.

These examples show that the political landscape may attract individuals seeking power to shield their immoral and illegal actions from scrutiny. The bipartisan nature of these scandals indicates that this issue transcends political ideology and speaks to a deeper corruption that pervades government. **How many unknown pedophiles work with impunity within the government?**

The disturbing reality is that allegations such as those raised by the Epstein and Pizzagate cases cannot be summarily dismissed without a thorough independent investigation. The suppression of evidence and the reluctance to hold individuals accountable point to a deliberate effort to protect those involved. As a society, dismissing these claims outright without addressing legitimate questions leaves the door open for continued abuse and systemic corruption. The evidence, from Epstein's extensive network to the arrests of elected officials for heinous crimes, demands transparency and accountability. Without it, society will continue on its path toward Tyranny.

Global Agendas

The possibility of international bodies of individuals and corporations orchestrating coordinated agendas has long sparked speculation and debate. Throughout history, there is clear evidence that, at times, groups dictate the changes that profoundly impact humanity, so the real question isn't if they exist but **what current groups should we be concerned about that are actively trying to alter human history to their needs and desires at the expense of ours?**

Recent developments by governments and international organizations lend credibility to the concerns that coordinated efforts are prioritizing globalist agendas over the rights and freedoms of individuals are underway. From sweeping policies like Agenda 2030 to financial tools like the Central Bank Digital Currencies (CBDC), these plans involve consolidating control in the name of addressing global challenges and disasters -even if they are manufactured crises. The idea of a coordinated global agenda should further be viewed as highly probable when we analyze the actions of influential asset management firms such as BlackRock and Vanguard as they amass unprecedented economic power and the secretive gatherings of the global elite during meetings like the Bilderberg Group and Bohemian Grove that meet without public accountability.

World Economic Forum – Agenda 2030

The WEF and its associated initiatives, such as Agenda 2030 and the Great Reset, illustrate a coordinated effort by an international network made up of over 1,000 members of corporations, governments, royalty, and industrial elites working together to centralize global power under the claim of addressing pressing global challenges and issues like climate change and economic inequality. Agenda 2030 -adopted by the U.N. and championed by the WEF- with its 17 SDGs, extends into nearly every facet of human life, including education, health, and economic systems, promising a future of equitable progress. This push to a "new world order" sparks fears of overreach and control, and rightfully so. While framed as philanthropic endeavors, these ambitious programs raise critical ethical and moral concerns about natural rights and autonomy on a global scale.

Agenda 2030 aims to align global efforts toward achieving sustainability, equity, and economic stability. This will be done by emphasizing and integrating advanced technology into global control and surveillance, aligning with the broader push for AI -for example, President Trump's AI Stargate Project- to play a central role in shaping the future. AI, positioned as a tool to enhance efficiency and address global challenges, is a fascinating and terrifying aspect of our future. Its implications for individual freedoms and rights are concerning. As highlighted in *The Age of AI: And Our Human Future* by Henry Kissinger, Eric Schmidt, and Daniel Huttenlocher (2021), AI enables mass surveillance, predictive policing, and data-driven control, equipping governments with unprecedented power and ability to suppress dissent and consolidate control. While these tools are framed as essential for security and humanity's progress, their implementation will likely reduce accountability and violate natural rights. The potential misuse of AI to enforce compliance raises serious questions about the ethical applications of the technology and the future it may shape.

Each of the 17 SDGs highlights different aspects of our lives that coordinated efforts are underway to take control and impose other individuals' wills upon us. For example, SDG 3, **Good Health and Well-being**, advocates for universal vaccinations, which threatens medical freedom and individual choice because, as seen with COVID19 during an emergency, the government will ignore and violate individual rights. The program's comprehensive scope, covering every aspect of public infrastructure, positions it as a framework for global governance, potentially undermining national sovereignty in the name of collective welfare. This has led many to question whether Agenda 2030 is a noble initiative or a pretext for consolidating power in the hands of a few at the cost of individual rights.

SDG 13, **Climate Action**, focuses on combating climate change and has been leveraged to justify policies that expand centralized control in the name of environmental protectors. One controversial example is the advocacy for lockdowns to address climate change, stressing how emergency measures can serve dual purposes. Lockdowns, initially justified as a response to COVID19, were later proposed by some as beneficial for the climate due to reduced carbon emissions during periods of restricted activity. On July 28th, 2020, RFK Jr. supported the rights violating COVID19 lockdowns, stating they provided an "opportunity" to address climate change by reducing human activity and its environmental impact. Ignoring the critical fallacious ideas in RFK Jr.'s stance, such proposals raise serious concerns about the potential for exploitation of natural or manufactured crises to promote policies that infringe on individual rights and impose sweeping social restrictions.

One emerging initiative aligning with Agenda 2030 is the concept of 15-minute smart cities, a framework designed to centralize urban living around walkable, tech-enabled neighborhoods where all daily needs - work, education, healthcare, and leisure- are accessible within a 15-minute radius. This concept has gained significant global traction, with numerous major cities pledging it as a goal, typically under the appearance of combating climate change and enhancing sustainability. Natural and manufactured crises, such as pandemics, wildfires, or climate emergencies, will be leveraged to justify these shifts, accelerating the social acceptance of 15-minute smart cities. Crises create a sense of urgency, allowing governments, institutions, and corporations to enforce sweeping social changes under the pretext of public safety and ecological responsibility. The result is a system that prioritizes control and compliance, aligning with the broader goals of Agenda 2030 to consolidate power and reshape society by building it back "better" after each crisis.

On day one of President Trump's second term, he established the Department of Government Efficiency (DOGE), which shows a potentially troubling trajectory toward centralized power and AI-driven control, falling squarely under SDG 16, **Peace, Justice, and Strong Institutions**. SDG 16 advocates for efficient and accountable institutions, yet DOGE could paradoxically expand governmental control and transfer key decision-making authority to AI systems to combat wasteful spending. Government is never efficient, and standing up a new alphabet agency is the opposite of reducing government overreach. While cloaked in the rhetoric of efficiency, DOGE risks becoming a mechanism for bloating bureaucracy, a move that should make us all wary of its true intentions. The potential for tyrannical expansion is a red flag that cannot be ignored.

Adding to the irony, the department's acronym -DOGE- is a tongue-in-cheek nod to Dogecoin, the cryptocurrency Musk advocated for starting in 2019, making the entire effort feel more like a calculated jest than a genuine movement around reform. As Musk's ventures in AI - OpenAI, Neuralink, etc.- aim to redefine how technology integrates with humanity -transhumanism- DOGE could become a testing ground for these systems under the guise of "efficiency." Instead of reducing inefficiencies, DOGE could drive further consolidation of power, align with globalist initiatives like Agenda 2030, and normalize AI control over critical societal functions. The potential loss of human judgment in favor of algorithms prioritizing efficiency over natural rights and freedoms is a cause for concern, leading the government toward Tyranny.

"Of liberty I would say that, in the whole plenitude of its extent, it is unobstructed action according to our will. But rightful liberty is unobstructed action according to our will within limits drawn around us by the equal rights of others. I do not add "within the limits of the law" because law is often but the tyrant's will, and always so when it

violates the rights of the individual." – Thomas Jefferson, *Letter to Isaac H. Tiffany* (April 4th, 1819)

Great Reset – Build Back Better

The WEF's push for a Great Reset, as articulated by Klaus Schwab -founder of WEF- envisions a transformation of capitalism, incorporating Marxist principles to create a globalized economic system driven by corporate-government partnerships. This envisioned overhaul of capitalism, leveraging crises like COVID19 to justify sweeping social and regulatory changes. Schwab's book *COVID-19: The Great Reset* outlines a shift toward Stakeholder Capitalism, where corporations supposedly act as trustees of society and the economy to address global challenges, which seems to be another tool and action of control. Similar to how past government operations, programs, and experiments are found out, names change, but the violations continue. This new version of controlled capitalism disrupts individual freedoms and property rights, consolidating power in the hands of unelected industrial elites under the appearance of sustainability and equity. The infamous 2016 WEF prediction for 2030, "You'll own nothing. And you'll be happy," epitomizes concerns about this centralized control and the direction we are being driven. **What sequenced events and crises must occur for everyone to own nothing and be happy by 2030?**

As promoted by the WEF, stakeholder capitalism prioritizes corporate governance over traditional free-market principles, effectively blending elements of socialism and state capitalism -crony capitalism. Individuals like Elon Musk are pushing this idea of stakeholder capitalism, which he is focused on helping usher in AI-driven transhumanistic societies. Rulers like President Biden and Prime Ministers Justin Trudeau -Canada- and Boris Johnson -United Kingdom- have also pushed this agenda through rhetoric like "Build Back Better," signaling alignment with Agenda 2030 goals. This coordinated effort threatens individual rights by using economic disruption and environmental concerns to justify increased government and corporate control over everyone's daily life.

Schwab's influence extends through initiatives like the Young Global Leaders program, a platform within the WEF that identifies and engages young leaders worldwide. This program has a network of prominent figures, including Prime Minister Trudeau and President Vladimir Putin, shaping policies worldwide, a key part of Schwab's strategy to influence global governance. His advocacy for integrating technology and government management into a transhumanist future illustrates the WEF's far-reaching ambitions. Schwab's controversial family ties, including his father's involvement in the Nazi war effort, add layers of controversy to his potential motivations and the organization's agenda, further fueling concerns about the implications of their envisioned future.

Environmental initiatives, such as the WEF's Investing in Forests campaign, illustrate the broader agenda's duality and mission scope. While promoting reforestation and climate action, these programs heavily rely on surveillance technologies like satellite monitoring and drones, raising concerns and fears of mass data collection and reduction of privacy standards and individual rights. With corporations like Microsoft, Google, and Amazon spearheading these efforts, we should question whether these tools serve the public good or pave the way for enhanced global surveillance control and a path toward Tyranny.

ID2020 – Central Bank Digital Currency

ID2020 -a global initiative uniting corporations, organizations, and governments- aims to provide digital IDs to billions of people worldwide. This aligns with the U.N.'s SDG 16, Peace, Justice and Strong Institutions, making it a significant player in the global digital identity landscape. Established in 2016 as a tax-exempt organization,

ID2020 is pioneering an international model for implementing digital ID solutions. It views identity as a fundamental human right to access social services, voting, and economic participation. ID2020 has formed strategic partnerships with entities like Microsoft, Accenture, GAVI, the Rockefeller Foundation, and Cisco Systems. These collaborations, including the one with the U.N. High Commissioner for Refugees (UNHCR) to draft The Alliance Manifesto, are designed to transcend national borders, affecting everyone. In the U.S., the Real ID Act of 2005 began aligning domestic policies with these global goals and efforts, paving the way for digital identification.

Digital IDs are not standalone innovations but part of a broader effort to create a fully traceable digital infrastructure. Central Bank Digital Currency (CBDC) represents a significant component of this system. On November 15th, 2022, the Federal Reserve Bank of New York, in partnership with Citigroup, HSBC, Mastercard, and Wells Fargo, launched a pilot program to explore a digital currency. This digital currency will be inherently traceable and controllable, lacking the decentralized freedom that defines most cryptocurrencies. When paired with digital IDs, CBDCs enable unprecedented surveillance and control over individuals' financial activities and actions, allowing governments to restrict access to funds and stifle opposition and disobedience while enforcing compliance. This level of centralized control poses a severe threat to individual rights and privacy.

Real-world examples emphasize how governments exploit digital financial systems to impose authoritarian policies. In December 2022, Nigeria's Central Bank limited daily ATM withdrawals to 20,000 nairas (approximately $45) and capped weekly over-the-counter withdrawals to push citizens toward a cashless economy reliant on digital currency. These measures serve as a reminder of the potential for governments to manipulate access to financial resources, coercing populations into adopting systems that increase government power and control. Similar tactics could be employed in the U.S. as the government pushes for broader CBDC adoption.

Integrating digital IDs and a CBDC raises alarming questions about their potential misuse. These systems will help pave the way for a dystopian future akin to China's social credit scoring system, where access to financial resources and social privileges is contingent upon government-approved behavior. The thought of a scenario where exceeding a monthly carbon dioxide allowance results in restricted access to funds or services should instill a sense of urgency and terror. Such a system will centralize control of every aspect of life into the hands of a few, with little room for dissent, disobedience, or non-compliance. The combination of digital IDs and CBDCs represents a slippery slope toward global surveillance and oppression, which are key aspects of a worldwide Tyranny.

Asset Corporations

BlackRock and Vanguard, with over $18 trillion in combined assets under management, effectively own significant stakes in nearly every primary industry: technology, healthcare, real estate, energy, etc. Their economic influence is unparalleled, with representation on the boards of countless corporations, enabling them to shape policies and strategies across all industries. These firms have aggressively acquired residential properties across the U.S., reducing housing availability and increasing prices and reliance on rental markets. This consolidation of assets in the hands of a few has exacerbated economic inequality. The concentration of wealth and power reshapes markets and encourages a system where public interests are subjugated to elite agendas.

In addition to controlling assets, BlackRock and Vanguard have leveraged their influence to shape rhetoric that serves their financial interests. For example, BlackRock has heavily invested in renewable energy technologies and climate infrastructure, industries projected to dominate global energy markets. To secure these investments, the corporation funneled millions into promoting the climate change rhetoric, funding initiatives such as Associated Press programs that hire climate-focused journalists to push the urgency of transitioning to green energy. Meanwhile, the corporations back politicians who vote for regulations favoring renewable energy while stifling traditional energy sources like coal and oil. Controlling the perceived problem and the forced marketed solution makes them significant profit.

This green energy shift is not without its drawbacks. The production of lithium and cobalt batteries, essential for renewable energy infrastructure, carries significant environmental and human costs, including habitat destruction and exploitative labor practices. The solutions offered by these entities ultimately worsen the issues they claim to address, raising questions about whether these efforts truly prioritize sustainability or merely serve to expand corporate dominance. BlackRock and Vanguard demonstrate how a small group can wield disproportionate influence over economies, policies, and public perceptions through their financial and rhetoric control. **Do you ever wonder why most products in the U.S. have toxic chemicals and dyes in food and drink that are banned in other countries? Who sits on those boards that make the products? Are toxins being purposely added to the food supply for more than greed?**

Secret Societies

The Bilderberg Group and Bohemian Grove illustrate two global elites' most prominent gatherings, creating suspicion about the actual purposes and agendas. The Bilderberg Group -formed in 1954- brings together approximately 130 influential figures annually, including political rulers, industry elites, royalty, and cultural influencers, to discuss global issues behind closed doors. No public records, votes, or resolutions are disclosed, leaving their activities shrouded in secrecy. This lack of transparency fuels speculation about the group's influence on policy decisions and social trends. Similarly, Bohemian Grove, an elite, invitation-only club founded in 1872, brings together influential individuals -including political rulers, royalty, and celebrities- for private retreats that have historically influenced significant events, such as the Manhattan Project -the development of the first nuclear weapon. Ritualistic events like the burning of a small coffin in front of a giant owl statue and rumors of debauchery only deepen the intrigue surrounding this group and clandestine gatherings.

Secret societies have long shaped historical and modern events. Freemasonry, one of the oldest and most prominent fraternal organizations, boasts millions of members worldwide and has included influential figures such as George Washington, Benjamin Franklin, and Ludwig van Beethoven. With origins in medieval stonemasonry, the organization's rituals and symbols have often been linked to broader power dynamics, cultivating suspicions about its influence on politics, culture, and religion.

The *Skull and Bones Society* at Yale University, also known as Order 322, is another example of how secret organizations permeate power structures. Founded in 1832, this society counts among its members U.S. Presidents William Taft, George H.W. Bush, and George W. Bush, further showing the direct influence of such groups on governance and policy. **It's a big club, and we aren't in it.**

The Bavarian Illuminati, though short-lived, remains a potent symbol of clandestine power. Founded in 1776 by Adam Weishaupt, this secret society sought to end monarchies and organized religion, replacing them with rational thought and a global republic. A "global republic" is a worldwide Tyranny with enough time -its natural lifecycle. After partnering with Freemasonry lodges to achieve its goals, the Illuminati reportedly dissolved in 1785 after internal conflicts. However, speculation about its continued existence has persisted, with other groups possibly co-opting its name. Its legacy has intertwined with modern conspiracy theories, fueled by symbols like the Eye of Providence, which appears on U.S. dollar prints and is linked to Freemasonry.

These groups, alongside entities like BlackRock and Vanguard, illustrate how concentrated wealth and power enable a select few to exert outsized influence on global governance, economies, and societies. Whether through private meetings, symbolic rituals, or systemic control over industries, these organizations and entities reinforce the idea of a hidden hierarchy directing social trends. Their secrecy and exclusivity perpetuate the rhetoric that a global elite operates with minimal accountability, prioritizing their interests, needs, and desires over individual rights and freedoms.

The overarching theme tying these conspiracy theories together reveals how all governments, through covert manipulation, systemic control, and exploitation, demonstrate a consistent progression toward Tyranny. From the historical roots of conspiracy theories to election interference, the execution of population control, global agendas, experimental practices on citizens, and secret societies, the pattern is unmistakable. Governments start with a semblance of freedom, gradually introducing measures and regulations that centralize power while destroying and suppressing any thought or idea of the importance of individual natural rights. This cycle perpetuates itself, leveraging crises and societal fears to take away freedoms and rights under the pretense of safety and progress. **It is for our safety!**

The trajectory is evident; consolidating power among global elites and asset corporations reflects a trend toward a tightly controlled tyranny worldwide. By dictating economic, political, and environmental rhetoric, governments and other entities reduce the power of individuals, fostering dependency, compliance, and approval of oppression. Moreover, experimental practices on citizens, coupled with a willingness to engage in or enable terrorism and violence, further solidify this shift. Whether through the overt actions of secret societies, covert intelligence operations, or programs like MKUltra and COVID19's live-fire exercise, governments repeatedly showcase their disregard for individual rights in pursuit of control and power. These patterns illustrate a historical and ongoing lifecycle where the result is Tyranny. Left unchecked, power inevitably leads to centralized tyranny and a violation of rights.

The fallacious belief in government as a necessary force is the root cause of the systemic issues that inevitably lead toward Tyranny. The very idea that this time, it will succeed keeps us in this perpetual lifecycle. By its very nature, governments derive power through coercion, manipulation, and control, violating the natural rights of individuals under the pretext of providing order and protection. This misplaced and blind trust and faith allow governments to grow unchecked, fostering corruption, prioritizing corporate and elite interests, and creating an illusion of choice through controlled opposition and co-opted movements.

History demonstrates that governments exploit crises to justify expanding authority and control. From mass surveillance to wealth redistribution schemes that benefit the few and from foreign interventions to authoritarian domestic policies, governments consistently consolidate power at the expense of the individual. The belief that government can solve the problems it creates blinds people to the reality that real progress lies in our evolution toward voluntary cooperation and exchange, autonomy, and facilitating systems rooted in natural rights and accountability -not centralized control. Without challenging this foundational fallacy, humanity remains trapped in an endless cycle of oppression, unable to evolve beyond being controlled and the constant path toward Tyranny.

"Where justice is denied, where poverty is enforced, where ignorance prevails, and where any one class is made to feel that society is an organized conspiracy to oppress, rob and degrade them, neither persons nor property will be safe." – Frederick Douglass, *West India Emancipation* (August 3rd, 1857)

Anarchism with Facilitating Systems

"Anarchism is not a romantic fable but the hardheaded realization, based on five thousand years of experience, that we cannot entrust the management of our lives to kings, priests, politicians, generals, and county commissioners." – Edward Abbey, *A Voice Crying in the Wilderness (Vox Clamantis en Deserto) : Notes from a Secret Journal* (1990)

Anarchism is misunderstood and misrepresented by government and mainstream media. Most do not understand its concepts or principles. It provides a radical option to the status quo and is a principled alternative to government. Contrary to the misconceptions perpetuated by governments and mainstream media, anarchism does not equate to chaos or lawlessness, as is the idea of barbarism. **'Anarchy'** means "without rulers" and "absence of government," emphasizing the absence of a government as explained throughout this book -*a tool or action of control*- over the innocent while promoting voluntary cooperation, mutual respect, and individual inherent natural rights. **'Anarchism'** is *a system and practice of no rulers, voluntary action, and an absence of government over the innocent based on natural rights -Life, Freedom, and Property*. It rejects the inherent tyranny in government -its nature- over the innocent. Instead, anarchism envisions free and organized communities functioning through facilitating systems that allow individuals to collaborate without the innocent needing to be controlled.

The idea of anarchy elicits strong reactions, usually fueled by a lack of understanding. The misconceptions of anarchy are primarily driven by government propaganda to sow hatred for the term anarchist, keeping the masses from understanding the term. Anarchy does not mean the absence of rules, principles, or leaders, nor does it imply the eradication of hierarchies or the destruction of property. The defining principle is the absence of rulers -those who use force and intimidation to control others. Conversely, leaders can exist in anarchist societies if followed voluntarily rather than by coercion and force. That is the difference between rulers and leaders, coercion and force, and the lack thereof.

Antifa, portrayed as an anti-fascist movement filled with self-proclaimed "anarchists," is a co-opted tool of governments, operating in ways that violate the very principles of anarchism Antifa claims to defend. By targeting and destroying the property of innocent individuals and businesses -while leaving the broader system of government power untouched- Antifa violates natural rights and contradicts the core ideals of anarchism. Their actions serve more as a PSYOP, designed to associate anarchist ideologies with chaos, violence, and destruction, effectively discrediting the philosophy of voluntaryism, rooted in the principle of non-aggression and the assertation that initiating force against an innocent -whether by an individual or an institution- is inherently unethical and immoral. By portraying themselves as agents of resistance while failing to challenge the overarching oppressive structures of government, Antifa purposely fortifies public reliance on government authority and discourages people from exploring anarchism as a legitimate, principled alternative to Tyranny.

Anarchism is a rich tapestry encompassing many schools of thought, such as Anarcho-Capitalism, Anarcho-Communism, Anarcho-Socialism, and Anarcho-Primitivism. While these disciplines may differ in focus and value, they share the fundamental belief in voluntary action and the absence of government control over the innocent. To me, being an anarchist means embracing all forms of anarchism that uphold the core principle of non-control. The most effective free and organized communities will draw from various schools of thought, incorporating their strengths to create a structure that facilitates daily life and social and community interactions. In such systems, all agreements must be entirely voluntary, reflecting a deep trust in individuals' capacity to govern themselves without the need for external force or coercion when victims have not been created -**no victim, no crime**.

Anarchism Schools of Thought

Anarchism is not a monolith; it encompasses diverse schools of thought, each reflecting a unique approach to achieving a governmentless society. However, within these modern movements that claim anarchism, many individuals lack a clear understanding of the principles that define anarchism. This leads to confusion and the rise of co-opted groups that dilute or distort the true essence of anarchism. At its heart, anarchism is a binary concept: it either upholds voluntary interactions -actions or agreements entered into willingly by all parties involved- and the absence of control or does not. There is no middle ground between anarchism and statism, between freedom and slavery. Any system or ideology that permits, condones, or perpetuates coercion and force over the innocent cannot claim to be anarchist in nature, regardless of how it brands itself. This rejection of coercion is a fundamental principle of genuine anarchism, ensuring the philosophy remains true to its ideals and principles.

Controlled opposition and confused statists claiming to represent anarchism exacerbate this problem. Groups that promote destruction, aggression, or involuntary redistribution under the banner of anarchism subvert the philosophy by aligning it with chaos and violence in the public eye. These distortions serve the interests of those in power, discrediting anarchism and discouraging people from exploring its true principles of peaceful, voluntary cooperation. It is vital to distinguish between genuine anarchism and its counterfeits, which only reinforce the chains of statism. This distinction empowers individuals to make informed choices about their beliefs and reassures them of anarchism's commitment to non-violence.

Anarcho-Capitalism

Anarcho-capitalism advocates for a governmentless society grounded in the natural rights of property and voluntary exchange. '**Capitalism**' is derived from the root definitions of '**capital**,' which means "property" or "resources," forming *a system and practice of trading property*. '**Property**' originates from the principle that individuals have an inherent claim to the fruits of their labor. The product of our labor -land, tools, or other resources- is our property, capital, and an extension of our autonomy.

This natural Right to Property also includes the freedom to exchange it voluntarily. Forced labor or the involuntary seizure of property of the innocent constitutes slavery, violating this core principle. In a free society, individuals can trade their labor or property for what they value more, whether through barter, trade, or a medium of exchange such as currency. For example, someone who raises chickens might trade surplus eggs with a butcher for meat or with another farmer for vegetables. Alternatively, they could trade the eggs for gold or silver, which might be used to buy tools or improve their land. This voluntary exchange enables individuals to specialize, create value, and fulfill their needs without coercion.

Anarcho-capitalism aligns with these principles by envisioning a society where free-market capitalism operates without interference from a government. It ensures that individuals maintain control over their property and the fruits of their labor. Free markets show how anarchist principles of freedom and non-aggression coexist with capital exchange, creating a society where individuals thrive through natural rights, fairness, and voluntary collaboration and exchange.

Anarcho-Communism

Anarcho-communism aims to create a society where resources and the means of production are held collectively, prioritizing communal ownership and mutual aid as the basis for economic and social organization. The term '**commune**' derives from the Latin *commūnis*, meaning "shared" or "common," emphasizing *a system and practice of shared responsibility and cooperation*. At its core, anarcho-communism seeks to eliminate hierarchical structures and private property ownership, replacing them with voluntary associations that manage resources and production collectively to meet the needs of all members of society.

In this vision, communal ownership means that the community collectively manages resources, ensuring equitable access without individual monopolization. Unlike the authoritarian interpretations of communism, which impose centralized control through coercive means, anarcho-communism operates through decentralized, voluntary networks. Decisions about resource allocation, production, and distribution are made collectively by those directly involved, cultivating a participatory system where all voices are heard, and no individual or group wields undue power over others. '**Personal possessions**' -items individuals use daily- are distinguished from '**private property**' - resources or assets hoarded for profit or power.

The practice of anarcho-communism aligns with anarchist principles by rejecting coercion and prioritizing voluntary cooperation. Under this structure, communities function as interconnected networks of mutual aid, where individuals contribute according to their abilities and receive according to their needs. This is said to create a sense of collective responsibility and interdependence. By grounding itself in the absence of rulers and the communal sharing of resources, anarcho-communism seeks to harmonize individual rights with collective well-being, offering a model of society that upholds individuality and solidarity. Those who wish to join and give up their property to the collective can do so voluntarily and leave when they no longer want to participate. If force becomes involved, it is no longer anarchism.

Anarcho-Socialism

Anarcho-socialism merges the principles of anarchism with the root concept of '**social**,' derived from the Latin *socius* meaning "companion" or "ally," representing *a system and practice of cooperative relationships within society*. It envisions a governmentless society where resources and wealth are collectively managed, prioritizing equity, mutual aid, and voluntary collaboration. This philosophy differentiates between '**personal property**' -possessions tied directly to individual use, such as homes, clothing, or tools, recognized as a natural right- and '**private property**' -resources or means of production owned for profit and control over others. Anarcho-socialists critique private property as a tool of exploitation and inequality, advocating for its replacement with collective stewardship of resources shared by those who use and depend on them.

Personal property is tied to individual autonomy and use. It aligns with natural rights by respecting the fruits of one's labor and possessions, directly supporting personal well-being. For example, while a home a family uses is personal property, a series of rental properties owned for profit and managed by "exploiting" tenants is classified as private property. Anarcho-socialists propose that collective ownership of such productive resources ensures equitable access and prevents the concentration of power and wealth in the hands of a few.

Anarcho-socialism champions decentralized systems, empowering workers and communities to self-manage resources and production through direct democracy and voluntary cooperation and exchange. For example, a collectively owned and managed farm would operate based on communal decisions about production and distribution, ensuring that resources meet collective needs without hierarchical authority or coercion. This system respects individual autonomy while supporting collective well-being, dismantling power hierarchies and exploitation by replacing profit-driven ownership with equitable resource sharing. Anarcho-socialism aligns with anarchist ideals and principles by rejecting coercion, prioritizing mutual aid, and ensuring that resources and wealth benefit all members of society while protecting personal property as an extension of natural rights. Those who wish to join and give up their property to the community can do so and then voluntarily leave when they no longer want to participate. As with the others, coercion and force cannot be used, or it isn't anarchism.

Anarcho-Primitivism

Anarcho-primitivism is a philosophy that critiques the foundations of modern industrial society and advocates for a return to a way of life rooted in simplicity, ecological harmony, and small-scale communities. The term '**primitive**,' derived from the Latin *primitivus*, means "first" or "original," emphasizing returning to fundamental, unaltered ways of living predating organized governments and industrialization. Anarcho-primitivists argue that the rise of complex hierarchies, technology, and industrial systems has alienated humanity from nature, driven inequality, and violated natural rights, including property rights tied to individual labor and use.

In anarcho-primitivism, property is understood as a natural right but contextualized within a subsistence-based, egalitarian structure. This means that '**personal possessions**,' such as tools, shelters, and clothing, are recognized as extensions of individual labor and immediate use, aligning with the principles of anarchism. However, '**private property**' -resources or land hoarded or controlled for profit or power- is rejected as an unnatural construct of industrial societies. Instead, anarcho-primitivists advocate for communal sharing of resources, emphasizing that the Earth's gifts, such as land and water, are meant to sustain all life rather than be monopolized by a few.

The practice of anarcho-primitivism envisions decentralized, non-hierarchical communities that subsist through hunting, gathering, and small-scale horticulture, rejecting industrialized production and the environmental destruction it entails. These communities prioritize cooperation, mutual aid, and a direct relationship with the natural world. For example, a group might collectively cultivate food, share resources like firewood or water, and create tools from available materials, promoting sustainability and minimizing exploitation. Without reliance on government or industrial systems, these communities maintain autonomy and self-sufficiency while fostering a strong sense of belonging and respecting the interconnectedness of all life.

This philosophy critiques modern civilization's alienating and destructive tendencies, such as overconsumption, environmental degradation, and social inequality, by emphasizing simplicity and a return to ecological balance. It proposes that true freedom and well-being lie in reconnecting with the rhythms of the natural world and dismantling systems that perpetuate inequality and environmental harm.

Voluntaryism and Libertarianism

Voluntaryism is the basis of anarchist philosophy. It emphasizes that all human interactions must be consensual and free from coercion and force. At its core, voluntaryism rejects the initiation of force -whether by individuals or entities- asserting that such aggression is inherently unethical and immoral. This principle forms the foundation of anarchist thought, advocating for a society where relationships and systems are rooted in autonomy, respect, and mutual informed consent.

In a voluntaryist society, all interactions are built on free and willing participation. Contracts and agreements are entered voluntarily, ensuring no one is coerced into unwanted obligations. Disputes are

Anarchism with Facilitating Systems

resolved through mutual consent or neutral arbitration rather than imposed by governments. Communities and markets thrive on reciprocity, enabling individuals to freely exchange goods, services, and ideas. Voluntaryism aligns seamlessly with anarchism, rejecting the use of force in favor of cooperative systems that uphold individual rights and conduct ethical collaboration.

Libertarianism and anarchism are deeply interconnected, with principled libertarians inherently aligning with anarchism. Libertarianism emphasizes key principles such as the Non-Aggression Principle (NAP) -which condemns the initiation of force except in self-defense, meaning that individuals have the right to defend themselves but not to initiate force against others- self-ownership -affirming individual self-governance over one's body and life- and property rights arising from labor and voluntary exchange. These values are the ethical and moral foundation of libertarian and anarchist thought.

Principled libertarians recognize that any form of government -as outlined in this book- even a limited one, violates these principles. Governments inherently rely on coercion to enforce laws, taxation, and regulations, contradicting the voluntary, non-aggressive ideals libertarians champion. Anarchists extend libertarianism to its logical conclusion by advocating for a governmentless society where participation, facilitation, justice, and mutual aid are entirely voluntary. In such a society, individuals freely form agreements, defend their rights, and manage communal resources without centralized authority, ensuring that freedom and autonomy are preserved.

Voluntaryism and anarchism offer a vision of a world where liberty and freedom are not compromised by coercion and relationships are defined by mutual respect and informed consent. By rejecting the inherent violence of the government, principled libertarians and anarchists champion a society that prioritizes freedom, ethical collaboration, and self-determination.

Facilitating Systems

Facilitatism offers a transformative alternative to traditional governance. It is *a system and practice of facilitating systems designed to coordinate and help solve problems through voluntary cooperation and exchange*. This is achieved through decentralized problem-solving, where decision-making and leadership are distributed among various levels of communities and organizations rather than concentrated in a single central authority with a monopoly on violence. In this context, "decentralized problem-solving" means that decision-making power is not held by a single entity but distributed among the community members. By creating an environment of accountability through recognized standards and certifications, facilitating systems empower communities to uphold natural rights and justice without relying on centralized forced control.

Facilitatism allows collaboration and conflict resolution without coercion and force, creating the groundwork for free and organized communities to thrive while protecting natural rights. By focusing on decentralized planning and problem-solving, dispute resolution, mutual aid, and free markets, facilitatism provides the functionality communities need to communicate and prosper, replacing the tools of control inherent in governments with cooperative voluntary exchange and just and equitable solutions. The idea of facilitatism emphasizes individual natural rights and supports industry standards, best practices, and certifications to ensure consistency, safety, and accountability across various communities.

For example, health and safety standards at restaurants set proper food handling, storage, and preparation techniques to protect consumers from preventable illnesses. A business is responsible for keeping customers and the public safe from their products and services. They must meet due diligence in that protection, or it can be considered criminal actions. Similarly, workplace safety regulations in manufacturing plants require protective equipment and machinery maintenance safeguards to prevent accidents and injuries. These industry standards create environments where individuals can operate and conduct business safely and confidently with established guidelines for due diligence. When incidents occur, these standards help distinguish between accidents and criminal negligence. This distinction plays a critical role in determining appropriate levels of restitution or criminal charges, which may include the loss of natural rights for those found to have willfully endangered others -creating victims.

Another example is the open-source technology movement, where individuals worldwide collaborate to create free tools, platforms, and systems that serve communal needs, free from coercive, centralized control. Projects like the Linux operating system, OpenStreetMap, and the Apache HTTP Server demonstrate how decentralized, voluntary cooperation can produce robust, widely-used systems that benefit everyone. Linux helps power the world's internet infrastructure and can come in many different versions, such as Ubuntu. Yet, it is developed and maintained by a global community of volunteers and contributors without the oversight of a coercive controlling authority. Similarly, OpenStreetMap provides detailed, user-generated maps accessible to anyone, outperforming commercial alternatives in certain areas. These initiatives and projects demonstrate how people can approach shared challenges, leveraging collective expertise to build systems that prioritize accessibility, transparency, and community-driven improvement without government coercion, regulations, and violence.

Facilitatism also includes community gardens, where individuals collaborate to cultivate food for their local areas. Community gardens are not just about growing food but about growing and developing communities. They typically are established in urban settings, providing fresh produce to neighborhoods while fostering a sense of community and shared responsibility. Participants voluntarily contribute their time, resources, and expertise to create a sustainable food source, addressing local needs without reliance on government programs or corporate intervention. Beyond the practical benefits, community gardens serve as hubs for education and connection, teaching participants about sustainable agriculture and encouraging deeper relationships among neighbors. By demonstrating how voluntary cooperation can address food security, scarcity, and the environmental challenges that arise, community gardens embody the principles of facilitatism, showcasing a grassroots approach to solving problems collectively and equitably.

Facilitatism is a beacon of empowerment, emphasizing that systems should empower individuals and communities rather than serve as instruments of control. It encourages decentralized solutions, allowing communities to address their unique challenges at the local level. This adaptability ensures that systems remain equitable, responsive, and aligned with the specific needs of the people they serve. More importantly, it supports a society where autonomy and collaboration are values and guiding principles. This empowerment is the key to a hopeful and inspiring future, where individuals and communities are not just passive recipients of governance but active participants in shaping their destinies.

Decentralized Problem-Solving

Decentralized problem-solving allows communities to lead themselves while collaborating on shared interests. Through direct collaboration, communities can make collective decisions via consensus or majority agreement, ensuring everyone's voice is heard and respected. Alternatively, autonomous groups can work together on broader issues, such as resource sharing or environmental protection, while maintaining independence. These decentralized models encourage cooperation on shared goals and ensure that decisions reflect each community's unique needs and values.

Facilitating systems plays a crucial role in promoting local autonomy and inclusivity. It can streamline community communication and collaboration, allowing them to coordinate efforts to address regional challenges through voluntary agreements and make collective decisions. For example, blockchain technology can create tokenized voting, consensus features and systems, and immutable record-keeping. This approach can ensure transparency, accountability, and inclusivity. It also ensures that leadership's direction remains grounded in mutual respect and self-determination.

Identity and Property Tracking

Identity and property tracking are foundational elements that ensure trust and prevent fraud in a decentralized system. These tools protect individual rights by clearly defining and protecting property ownership. For example, blockchain technology provides an immutable and decentralized ledger, recording ownership and transactions with transparency and security. By verifying identities and ensuring that property transfers occur only with full informed consent, such systems eliminate ambiguities and reduce the potential for disputes or fraudulent claims. This helps prevent a community member from having their property or identity stolen, which is a violation of rights.

Dispute Resolution

Conflicts are a natural part of human interaction, but their resolution typically does not necessitate the coercive intervention of a government. Facilitating systems provide alternative methods, such as arbitration and mediation, where neutral third parties assist in finding fair and mutually agreeable outcomes for all involved. These approaches prioritize voluntary participation and respect for individual autonomy, ensuring that solutions are collaborative rather than imposed. Restorative justice takes this further by focusing on repairing harm and rebuilding relationships, emphasizing accountability and reconciliation over punishment. By cultivating dialogue and understanding, these systems uphold the principles of fairness and community cohesion while avoiding the punitive and inequitable measures characteristic of traditional legal systems.

Mutual Aid and Resource Sharing

Facilitating systems can help prioritize mutual aid, building a culture where individuals and groups voluntarily pool their resources and skills to address shared and complex challenges. This collaborative approach allows communities to address collective needs without relying on coercive structures or bureaucratic inefficiencies. For example, community cooperatives can manage essential services such as healthcare, education, and infrastructure projects, tailoring them to local needs and values. These cooperatives operate on principles of shared ownership and problem-solving, ensuring that those directly affected by these services have a voice in their development and implementation.

Grassroots disaster relief networks are a shining example of the power that mutual aid brings to communities. In times of crisis, these networks can mobilize resources and respond to emergencies more efficiently than sizeable government agencies that are slowed by red tape and centralized authority dictating unethical and immoral decisions and actions. Local knowledge, decentralized coordination, and voluntary contributions enable facilitating networks to act swiftly and adaptively, addressing immediate needs while building resilience for the future. Mutual aid strengthens social bonds and builds trust by empowering communities to take responsibility for their welfare and safety. It ensures that resources are directed where they are most needed without imposing control or infringing individual autonomy and rights.

Free Markets and Exchange

Markets flourish under the principles of voluntaryism, where all exchanges are based on mutual consent and provide value to all participants. In such systems, the absence of coercion or force ensures that transactions are fair and that individuals can choose how, when, and with whom they trade. This creates a marketplace driven by confidence, credibility, innovation, and genuine need rather than manipulation or exploitative practices. The fairness and transparency of voluntaryism reassure participants and instill confidence in the system, making them feel secure and confident.

Reputation networks are crucial in maintaining accountability and building trust in voluntary markets. By allowing individuals and businesses to construct transparent records of their behavior, these systems empower participants to make informed decisions about whom to engage with. For example, peer-reviewed ratings and feedback can showcase reliable sellers, ethical practices, and quality products while discouraging dishonesty and exploitation. Such networks incentivize ethical conduct and create a self-regulating environment that replaces the need for intrusive government oversight and tyranny, making participants feel secure and protected.

Decentralized currencies, including cryptocurrencies like Bitcoin and Ethereum, provide a secure, transparent, and borderless means of exchange, free from governments and the control of centralized financial institutions. Barter systems offer another alternative, enabling direct trade of goods and services, particularly in local or resource-constrained settings. Together, these systems empower individuals to engage in commerce on their terms, boosting economic independence and resilience while preserving the principles of voluntaryism and self-ownership.

Government Over Criminals

The only justification for government, *a tool and action of control* - not the oppressive, tyrannical system over the innocent as seen today- lies in its ability to address criminal behavior. Criminals are not innocent. Criminal actions result in clear harm and victimization of the innocent. A society's sense of justice depends on identifying and addressing wrongs where individuals or groups infringe upon others' rights. In this context, the only possible legitimate role of government is to act as an instrument of control and justice and facilitating system in controlling criminal behavior, ensuring that those who create victims face the consequences and owe restitution while respecting the autonomy and natural rights of the innocent. The principle is simple: **no victim, no crime**. This principle means that the government should only intervene when there is an apparent victim, with the role of "government" limited to addressing these examples of harm.

True crime requires the presence of a victim -someone whose natural rights to Life, Freedom, or Property have been violated. Theft, assault, fraud, and similar offenses all create victims by infringing upon their ability to live freely and securely. These actions disrupt the social fabric and necessitate a response to restore balance and protect others from further harm. Conversely, victimless actions, such as personal lifestyle choices or voluntary exchanges, do not create harm or infringe upon others' rights. Labeling such acts as crimes represents an overreach of authority and statism, diverting resources from addressing genuine harm, creating unnecessary control over individuals' lives, and moving to a system that is built around and supports Tyranny.

The **no victim, no crime** principle aligns with natural rights, emphasizing that individuals are free to live as they choose, provided their actions do not harm others. This principle inherently limits the scope of authority, preventing an institution from infringing on individual rights under the pretext of maintaining order. A facilitating system should address genuine harm caused by criminal actions, not regulate individual behavior or enforce arbitrary rules that impose control over the innocent, leading to slavery and Tyranny.

Humanity stands at a pivotal crossroads, confronting the philosophical challenges of systemic corruption, engineered crises, and the direct attack on natural rights under the excuse of progress and security. The history of government as a tool or action of control, rooted in coercion and force and veiled in benevolent rhetoric, consistently cycles through Tyranny. To break free from this endless loop, we must embrace the philosophy of **Evolution, not Revolution**, striving toward a societal transformation rooted in voluntary cooperation and exchange, mutual respect, and decentralization. Revolution resets the cycle of government but retains the structures that perpetuate oppression and statism. Evolution offers the chance to transcend this insanity.

As they exist, governments prioritize control over facilitation, substituting individual autonomy with perceived authority, justified by the need to address natural and manufactured societal problems. This paradigm ensures dependence, disempowers individuals, and allows unchecked corruption to thrive. The only legitimate function of government authority -addressing crimes that harm others, turning them into victims- has been obscured by layers of fallacious beliefs, engineered consent, and manufactured crises that drive fear and a willingness to give up rights. The televised "revolutions" we are encouraged to rally behind are tools for further entrenching power, ensuring the status quo of centralized control. Yet, a more hopeful path exists, grounded in facilitatism and anarchism.

Anarchism and facilitatism offer a blueprint for governmentless societies where decentralized systems support individual autonomy and communal collaboration. This vision prioritizes anarchism and voluntaryism, ensuring interactions are consensual and free from coercion while respecting natural rights -protecting Life, Freedom, and Property. Through decentralized networks, communities can make decisions reflecting their unique needs and values while leveraging cooperative systems for broader challenges. Identity confirmation and property tracking ensure confidence and fairness, preventing exploitation and fraud without authoritarian oversight. Tools like blockchain can record transactions transparently, upholding individual ownership and enabling accountability.

Conflict resolution can shift from punitive systems to restorative practices that repair harm and provide reconciliation. Mutual aid networks, community cooperatives, and grassroots disaster responses can replace bureaucratic inefficiency with compassionate and immediate support. Free markets, grounded in voluntary exchange and decentralized currencies, ensure trade flourishes without manipulation by corrupt governments and centralized financial institutions. These systems should be designed to enable rather than control and embody a structure where humanity can evolve beyond the need for imposed authority and control.

The current trajectory for all citizens in the world points toward a new **Age of Tyranny**, marked by global surveillance, engineered dependence, and the consolidation of power into the hands of a select few. Initiatives like the Great Reset and digital ID systems under Agenda 2030 aim to centralize control under the pretext of addressing global crises that are most likely manufactured. The COVID19 pandemic, supply chain disruptions, and economic manipulations have demonstrated how crises can be exploited to strip freedoms and rights, transfer wealth upward, and implement authoritarian measures and restrictions. These engineered steps reflect a carefully designed path to further subjugation and drive the world toward Tyranny.

Yet, this does not have to be our future. Tyranny thrives on compliance, fear, and a lack of awareness. Humanity can break free from these chains by choosing defiance in the face of statism and reclaiming autonomy and self-determination. The answer lies not in passive acceptance or violent upheaval but in evolutionary resistance - using systems that empower individuals and communities to govern

Anarchism with Facilitating Systems 175

themselves without coercion. However, the situation's urgency may sometimes necessitate evolutionary jumps that require chaos and violence to drive humanity toward a different path and fundamental understanding. True freedom is rooted in knowledge, self-determination, the courage to reject oppressive systems, and the willingness to fight against a tyrannical entity to protect natural rights.

The ability to predict the course of humanity's path, much like anticipating moves in chess, hinges on understanding patterns and the factors influencing them. The patterns of tyranny, rebellion, and repression -purposely not being aware of difficult thoughts, memories, or feelings- are well-documented, but so are the moments of compassion, innovation, and transformation that have always pushed humanity forward. The future is not predetermined; it is shaped by the choices we and others make and the actions we take to the changes happening around us. We can steer humanity toward a freer, more equitable future by rejecting fear and Tyranny, embracing critical thought through the Trivium, and encouraging anarchism through facilitating systems.

The call is clear: We must resist the seduction of false choices and controlled opposition, challenge the rhetoric that justifies oppression, and actively build systems rooted in autonomy, collaboration, and justice. The belief in government as a necessary or benevolent institution of evil and control is a fallacy. Governments thrive on the illusion of necessity, yet history demonstrates that their existence consistently leads to corruption, exploitation, and the destruction of individual natural rights.

The road ahead is steep and highly dangerous. Still, the potential for a brighter future lies in rejecting this belief in government as a fallacy, defying the cycles of Tyranny, and embracing self-determination and voluntary cooperation and exchange. By building systems that uphold natural rights and seek true justice, humanity can transcend the need for imposed authority and control and create a world free from oppression while choosing the clear path forward: **Evolution, not Revolution.**

"I consider that in no government power can be abused long. Mankind will not bear it. If a sovereign oppresses his people to a great degree, they will rise and cut off his head. There is a remedy in human nature against tyranny, that will keep us safe under every form of government."
– Samuel Johnson, *in conversation with Sir Adam Fergusson, James Boswell Life of Johnson (Oxford: OUP, 1989)* (March 31st, 1772)

About the Author

"Never let the future disturb you. You will meet it, if you have to, with the same weapons of reason which today arm you against the present."
– Marcus Aurelius, *Meditations, Book VII* (170 to 180 AD)

Every individual is a complex tapestry of experiences and values, far more intricate than the labels or descriptors they might use to define themselves. While such terms can help find like-minded individuals or provide a glimpse into someone's principles, they only scratch the surface of a person's experiences and values. For example, I describe myself as an anarchist, voluntarist, principled libertarian, philosopher, conspiracy theorist, U.S. Army veteran, business and solutions analyst, data analyst, cyber analyst, intelligence analyst, legislative analyst, graphics and website designer, network and systems administrator, content creator, writer, journalist, author, vaccine risk-aware advocate, son, husband, and father. While these labels offer insight, they cannot fully encapsulate the depth of my experiences or the principles that guide my life.

I live by principles that uphold natural rights -Life, Freedom, and Property- for all, navigating an unjust and corrupt system to the best of my ability. The Trivium Method of Critical Thinking -rooted in Grammar, Logic, and Rhetoric- has shaped my understanding of anarchism as the most ethical and logical framework for free and organized community structures. Anarchism, usually misunderstood, is a beacon of hope that vehemently rejects Tyranny while embracing voluntary cooperation and exchange, mutual respect, and self-governance. It is not chaos or the absence of rules but faith in humanity's ability to coexist freely without rulers. To break free from

About the Author

the endless cycle of government-imposed tyranny, humanity must evolve toward this vision of freedom and embrace its capacity for self-governance.

The term 'anarchy' typically triggers strong reactions due to widespread misconceptions. At its core, anarchy means "without rulers" -the absence of government- not the absence of order or principles. True anarchism rejects coercion while respecting natural rights such as property and the autonomy of individuals. It recognizes that rules, hierarchies, and leadership can emerge naturally through voluntary participation rather than imposed authority. Groups like Antifa, misrepresented as anarchists, violate these principles through coercion and destruction, demonstrating a sophist misunderstanding of anarchism. True anarchism is rooted in voluntary cooperation, exchange, and trust in individuals to govern themselves, ensuring a safe and respectful society.

Anarchism encompasses diverse schools of thought, and while I respect these approaches when they remain voluntary, I do not subscribe to any single school of thought. My vision of anarchism is broader, rejecting all forms of coercive control over the innocent. Any agreement or system built on voluntary participation aligns with this philosophy. Guided by a logical pursuit of truth and respect for natural rights, I advocate for communities free from imposed authority over the innocent.

With over a decade of experience as a Product, Solutions, and Business Analyst in software development, six years in the U.S. Army as an Infantryman and Cyber Intelligence Analyst, and five years as a Network and Systems Administrator, I have developed a deep understanding of systems and structures that can help free and organized societies function. My formal education includes a Master of Business Administration (MBA) in IT Management, a Bachelor of Arts (BA) in Liberal Arts, multiple Associate of Science (AS) degrees (Computer Engineering, Intelligence Operations, and Digital Media), and ongoing work toward a Master of Science (MS) in Data Analytics focusing on

Decision Process Engineering. These experiences have given me the tools to critically analyze complex data and systems and advocate for a world rooted in autonomy, justice, and mutual respect.

Throughout my life, I have pursued truth and stood against injustice, even when it placed me at odds with family, friends, and social norms. This unwavering commitment has led to censorship and backlash, particularly when challenging mainstream rhetoric. Nevertheless, I continue to speak out for the innocent whose rights are violated. Anarchism is not about rejecting order; it is about rejecting Tyranny and building a world where individuals coexist freely through voluntary cooperation and exchange. I hope my work inspires others to envision and strive for a freer and more just future as I picture it can be.

I can currently be found and contacted through the following locations and accounts:
- Email
  - JeffreyHann@protonmail.com
- Website
  - https://www.journalisticrevolution.com
- Facebook
  - https://www.facebook.com/JournalisticRevolution
- Instagram
  - https://www.instagram.com/jeffrey.a.hann
  - https://www.instagram.com/journalisticrevolution
- Minds
  - https://www.minds.com/jeffreyhann/
- Steemit
  - https://steemit.com/@jeffreyahann
- Substack
  - https://jeffreyhann.substack.com/
- Telegram
  - https://t.me/JournalisticRevolution
  - https://t.me/WelcomeToTheCollapse

About the Author

- X (formerly Twitter)
  - https://x.com/JeffHannMADA

Here is a list of all of my free published work:
- March 15th, 2016: *Why taxation is theft*
  - https://journalisticrevolution.com/why-taxation-is-theft.html
- July 21st, 2016: *What is a Police Enforcement Officer and what are their duties with regards to our rights?*
  - https://journalisticrevolution.com/what-is-a-police-enforcement-officer-and-what-are-their-duties-with-regards-to-our-rights.html
- August 16th, 2016: *Know your grammar, what is terrorism?*
  - https://journalisticrevolution.com/know-your-grammar-what-is-terrorism.html
- September 5th, 2016: *What made America great?*
  - https://journalisticrevolution.com/what-made-america-great.html
- December 24th, 2016: *Remember Remember Remember*
  - https://journalisticrevolution.com/remember-remember-remember.html
- January 5th, 2017: *Why I am a Libertarian and Anarchist, by definition*
  - https://journalisticrevolution.com/why-i-am-a-libertarian-and-anarchist-by-definition.html
- August 1st, 2017: *Taxation is theft, by definition*
  - https://journalisticrevolution.com/taxation-is-theft-by-definition.html
- September 18th, 2017: *Conspiracy Theory: Government and Central Banking lies about Bitcoin - CEO of JPMorgan and Director of the Federal Reserve Jamie Dimon commits fraud*
  - https://journalisticrevolution.com/conspiracy-theory-government-and-central-banking-lies-about-bitcoin.html
- July 11th, 2019: *To Vaccinate or Not to Vaccinate: Informed Consent*
  - https://journalisticrevolution.com/to-vaccinate-or-not-to-vaccinate-informed-consent.html
- May 29th, 2020: *COVID1984: A Plandemic Love Story (Part 1)*
  - https://journalisticrevolution.com/covid1984-a-plandemic-love-story-part-1.html
- May 29th, 2020: *COVID1984: A Plandemic Love Story (Part 2)*

About the Author

- o   https://journalisticrevolution.com/covid1984-a-plandemic-love-story-part-2.html
- April 17th, 2022: *IN-DEPTH ANALYSIS OF COVID19: The Truth Is Out There*
  - o   https://journalisticrevolution.com/in-depth-analysis-of-covid19-the-truth-is-out-there.html
- April 12th, 2023: *Human Things Poem*
  - o   https://journalisticrevolution.com/human-things-poem.html
- November 13th, 2024: *The Fallacious Belief in Government* (Presentation)
  - o   https://journalisticrevolution.com/the-fallacious-belief-in-government.html

Movie Producer Credits:
- *The Monopoly on Violence* (2020) – Documentary
  - o   https://www.imdb.com/title/tt10627868/
- *Overpoliced* (2021) – Documentary
  - o   https://www.imdb.com/title/tt13828586/

Published Books:
- February 21st, 2023: *COVID19 – SHORT PATH TO 'YOU'LL OWN NOTHING. AND YOU'LL BE HAPPY.': Welcome to the new Age of Tyranny*
  - o   https://journalisticrevolution.com/published-books.html

Author Page

Fallacious Belief in Government presentation

About the Author

Meet the future with confidence and determination